Concurrentes	Littere dominicales	Ebdomade a natali usque ad invocavit 6	7	8	9	10	11	[illegible]	Ā	7
6	a		f	u	b	g	o	[illegible]	6	6
5	b		g	o	a	h	p	1	5	5
4	c		h	p	b	i	q	2	4	4
3	d	b	i	q	c	k		3	3	3
2	e	c	k	r	d	l		4	2	2
1	f	d	l	s	e	m		5	1	1
7	g	e	m	t	f	n		6		
Ebdomade a pentecoste ad adventum domini		29	28	27	26	25	24			
Ebdomade a pentecoste ad festum johannis		6	5	4	3	2	1			

The Christian Calendar
and the Gregorian Reform

The CHRISTIAN CALENDAR and the GREGORIAN REFORM

Peter Archer, S.J.
Canisius College, Buffalo, N. Y.

FORDHAM UNIVERSITY PRESS
NEW YORK

First Edition. Mss.

IMPRIMI POTEST

JAMES J. SWEENEY, S.J.
Provincial, Maryland-New York

NIHIL OBSTAT

ARTHUR J. SCANLAN, S.T.D.
Censor deputatus

IMPRIMATUR

✠ FRANCIS J. SPELLMAN, D.D.
Archbishop of New York

May 20, 1941

Printed in the United States of America

To the

SOCIETY of JESUS

on the

Fourth Centenary

of its

Foundation

PREFACE

Of the many ways of reckoning time, the Christian calendar is the most widespread; it is of interest to all, for like a wrist-watch it is frequently consulted in the regulation of our lives.

The mathematical equipment needed for its study is very moderate. Yet its problems are not easy. Simple as the calendar is in its daily application, it is remarkable how elusive it becomes when projected into the distant future, or referred to the remote past. This is particularly true of its lunar part.

The following pages contain a study of the Christian luni-solar calendar and of its Gregorian correction. The study originated in an attempt at improvement and ended with the recognition of a masterpiece. Incidentally these pages present a history of that calendar from before the beginning of the Christian Era. Not a few of the formulas and tables are new; it is hoped that their application will be found easy and convenient.

The book should prove useful for historians, for private reading, for study clubs, for the reference shelves in libraries, or as a text for a short course on the calendar in colleges and seminaries.

CONTENTS

LIST OF TABLES

The Christian Calendar

and the Gregorian Reform

The Christian Calendar and the Gregorian Reform

Section 1

The Christian Era. Its first year.

The idea of a Christian Era originated with Dionysius Exiguus, a monk living at Rome in what is now called AD 527. He figured back to what he regarded as the beginning of Christ's life on earth. Modern scholarship, for historical reasons, places the birth of Christ about seven years earlier.

The first year of the New Era was styled AD 1. The use of the zero in computations was then unknown, the Roman notation having no symbol for it. The year preceding AD 1 is ordinarily called BC 1 by historians.

However, for the purpose of this study, the year immediately preceding AD 1 will be called AD 0, and will be regarded as the first year of the Christian Era. This convention has several advantages:

(1) A century is now commonly thought to begin with the zero-year in its hundred. Thus the twentieth century, or the nineteen-hundreds, began with AD 1900; consistently, the first century or the zero-hundreds should begin with the year AD 0; else we should have the anomaly of one of the centuries, the first, containing only 99 years. Historical dates are usually given in terms of years, months, and days; but a date of this first year of the Era would have been given in terms of months and days only—just as the age of an infant in its first year is given in terms of months and days.

(2) Many formulas, as we shall see, can be more easily derived and applied on the assumption that *every* century, including the first, began with the zero-year in its hundred.

The year AD 0 was a leap* year, like AD 4, 8, 12, etc. In a leap year the intercalary day compensates for the decimal part of a day annually omitted from the solar calendar during the preceding four years; it brings the solar calendar up to date.

Two elements for any given year are important in calendar work: the golden number and the dominical letter.

* The name arose as follows. March was formerly the first month of the English year. Successive years ordinarily began on successive days of the week; but owing to the extra day that had been added in February, every fourth year began *two* days later in the week than the preceding year, thus seeming to *leap* over one day of the week. With the transfer of the year's beginning to January, the name ceased to be appropriate, but it was retained.

SECTION 2

Golden Numbers

IF ALL TIME is divided into cycles of nineteen calendar years each, the golden number (GN) for a given year is defined as the number of that year in its cycle. This number was called golden, either because of its importance in the lunar calendar, as one speaks of a *golden* opportunity, or because the ancient Athenians were so proud of the discovery of this nineteen-year cycle that they engraved the current year's number in figures of gold on a pillar in the agora, as one of the glories of Athens.

The GN for any year of the Christian Era is found by adding *one* to the remainder (R) after the number of the given year in the Era is divided by 19. One must be added to R because the year AD 0 was the year 1 in its golden number cycle. The quotient is of no importance, because, in the Christian calendar, the cycles are not counted.

The beginning of such a system of 19-year cycles was *arbitrary*, but once chosen, the system remains constant until it is deliberately changed. Hence, it is not surprising that the golden number in the Jewish calendar differs from the Christian golden number for any given year. The relation is:

$$\text{Jewish GN} + 2 = \text{Christian GN}$$

Examples: Find the GN for the years:

(1) AD 1935.	We have:	$1935 \div 19$ leaves	$R = 16$.	GN =	$(16 + 1)$ or 17
(2) AD 856.	" "	$856 \div 19$ "	$R = 1$.	GN =	$(1 + 1)$ or 2
(3) AD 855.	" "	$855 \div 19$ "	$R = 0$.	GN =	$(0 + 1)$ or 1
(4) AD 0.	" "	$0 \div 19$ "	$R = 0$.	GN =	$(0 + 1)$ or 1

SECTION 3

Dominical letters and numbers. Formulas for finding them. Construction of a table for the same purpose.

IF THE FIRST seven letters of the alphabet are assigned successively to the calendar dates of the year, beginning with A on Jan 1, the dominical letter (DL) for a given year is defined as the letter that will indicate on an ecclesiastical yearly calendar (Table IX) which calendar dates of that year are Sundays.

For computation purposes, we substitute *dominical numbers* (DN), by letting the numbers 1 to 7 stand for the first seven letters of the alphabet, so that 1 stands for A, 2 for B, etc., and 7 for G.

The dominical number for any given year of the Christian Era, the year beginning on Jan 1, in the absence of a suitable table, may be found by one of the following simple formulas:

To Oct 4, 1582	$\mathrm{DN} = 10 - \left(6\mathrm{H} + \mathrm{Y} + \frac{\mathrm{Y}}{4}\right)$	I
From Oct 15, 1582	$\mathrm{DN} = 8 - \left(5\mathrm{H} + \frac{\mathrm{H}}{4} + \mathrm{Y} + \frac{\mathrm{Y}}{4}\right)$	II

where H is the hundred-number in the given year, and Y is the year's number in its hundred; thus, in AD 1451, H is 14, and Y is 51.

In applying these new formulas, exact multiples of 7 may be omitted or added wherever convenient, except in the numerator of a fractional term, such as $\frac{\mathrm{H}}{4}$; on division by 4, the remainder is disregarded.

In *leap* years, the DN found by either formula is the one current after the intercalary day; to find the DN current before, and on the intercalary day, the DN found by the formula must be *increased* by one.

In the ecclesiastical calendar, the intercalary day in leap years is on Feb 24; in the civil calendar it is Feb 29. (See *Section 21.*)

Examples: Find the dominical letters for the years:

(1)	AD 1451*	By I: $\mathrm{DN} = 10 - (0 + 2 + 5) = 3$;	DL is C
(2)	AD 1452 (leap year)	By I: $\mathrm{DN} = 10 - (0 + 3 + 6) =$ 1 or A, 2 or B	DL is BA
(3)	AD 0 (leap year)	By I: $\mathrm{DN} = 10 - (0 + 0 + 0)$; 3 or C, 4 or D	DL is DC
(4)	AD 1935	By II: $\mathrm{DN} = 8 - (4 + 4 + 0 + 1)$; 6	DL is F
(5)	AD 1936 (leap year)	By II: $\mathrm{DN} = 8 - (4 + 4 + 1 + 2)$; 4 or D, 5 or E	DL is ED
(6)	AD 3170	By II: $\mathrm{DN} = 8 - (1 + 0 + 0 + 3)$; 4	DL is D
(7)	AD 3700 (common year)	By II: $\mathrm{DN} = 8 - (3 + 2 + 0 + 0)$; 3	DL is C
(8)	AD 1582 to Oct 4.	By I: $\mathrm{DN} = 10 - (6 + 5 + 6)$; 7	DL is G
	AD 1582 from Oct 15.	By II: $\mathrm{DN} = 8 - (5 + 3 + 5 + 6)$; 3	DL is C

From the last example one sees that the omission of ten days from the calendar in AD 1582, while not interfering with the sequence of the days of the week, *did* interfere with the sequence of the dominical letters.

* In applying the formula to this example, the successive terms are: 6 $(14 - 2 \times 7) = 0$; $51 - 7 \times 7 = 2$; $\frac{51}{4} - 7 = 5$, where the remainder 3 is disregarded. Similarly in succeeding applications.

1° Proof of *Formula I*.

One common year ends with an excess (over the highest multiple of seven days) of one day, because

$$365 = 52 \times 7 + 1;$$

one hundred common years end with an excess of 100 days.

Since in the Old Style (OS) calendar to Oct 4, 1582, *every* fourth year was a leap year, one hundred OS years, due to the 25 intervening leap years, end with an excess of 125, or 6 days; and H hundred years end with an excess of 6H days. Similarly Y years accumulate in the century an excess of $\left(Y + \frac{Y}{4}\right)$ days. Therefore (H hundred and Y)* OS years *end* with an excess of $\left(6H + Y + \frac{Y}{4}\right)$ days.

Now, in any calendar year, whether Old Style or New Style, such as the year 1939, the year 1900 is *preceded* by 19 hundred years, the zero-hundred being the first; the year 39 is preceded in its century by 39 years, the first being the zero-year in its hundred.

Therefore, any given OS year—the year (H hundred and Y), *began* at midnight preceding Jan 1, with an excess of $\left(6H + Y + \frac{Y}{4}\right)$ days. This excess, after omitting sevens, is as yet unrelated to the days of the week; it is made to begin with the first day of the week (Sunday) by the addition of a *constant* number Q, whose value depends on the initial condition at the beginning of the Christian Era. So that, when the given OS year began, the week† was

$$\left(6\,H + Y + \frac{Y}{4} + Q\right)$$

days old and there remained

$$7 - \left(6\,H + Y + \frac{Y}{4} + Q\right)$$

days to the end of the week (Saturday night) in the given year.

Therefore $$8 - \left(6\,H + Y + \frac{Y}{4} + Q\right) = DN$$

for that year.

* Note the difference between a general interval of (H hundred and Y) years, and the year (H hundred and Y); between 1939 years and the year 1939.

† The word "week" has two meanings: 1° A group of *any* seven consecutive days, as when New Year's day is said to be one week later than Christmas; 2° A group of seven consecutive days beginning with Sunday and ending Saturday night. It is so used here.

The value of the constant Q may be found from some *known* OS common year date, such as Thursday, Oct 4, 1582; the position of Thursday, Oct 4, in Table IX shows that DL was G, or DN was 7

Thus, $$8 - (6 + 5 + 6 + Q) = 7$$

and therefore $$Q = 5$$

By substitution above, we have for any OS common year:

$$DN = 10 - \left(6\,H + Y + \frac{Y}{4}\right) \quad \textit{Q.e.d.}$$

2° Proof of *Formula II*

The proof is quite similar to the preceding. In the New Style (NS) calendar beginning with Oct 15, 1582, century years, unless multiples of 400, are common years. For the purpose of this proof, it is assumed that this Gregorian Rule had been in force from the beginning of the Christian Era, in which assumption no attention need be paid to the calendar reform of AD 1582; a reform would never have become necessary.

One hundred NS years end with an excess of (100 + 24), or 5 days, there being only 24 leap years in an ordinary century. H hundred years end with an excess of $\left(5\,H + \frac{H}{4}\right)$ days, because of the century leap years. Hence, any given NS year, such as the year (H hundred and Y), *begins* with an excess of $\left(5\,H + \frac{H}{4} + Y + \frac{Y}{4}\right)$ days.

This excess is made to begin on a Sunday by the addition of a constant number S, whose value depends, both on the initial condition at the beginning of the Christian Era, and on the omission of ten dates from the calendar, and the substitution of Formula II for Formula I in AD 1582.

So that, when the given NS year begins, the week is

$$\left(5\,H + \frac{H}{4} + Y + \frac{Y}{4} + S\right)$$

days old, and there remain

$$7 - \left(5\,H + \frac{H}{4} + Y + \frac{Y}{4} + S\right)$$

days to the end of the week (Saturday night) in the given year.

Therefore $$8 - \left(5\,H + \frac{H}{4} + Y + \frac{Y}{4} + S\right) = DN$$

for that year.

The value of the constant S may be found from some *known* NS common year date, such as Friday, Oct 15, 1582; the position of Friday, Oct 15 in Table IX shows that DL was C, or DN was 3.

Thus $$8 - (5 + 3 + 5 + 6 + S) = 3$$

and therefore $$S = 7 \text{ or } 0$$

By substitution above, we have for any NS common year:

$$DN = 8 - \left(5\,H + \frac{H}{4} + Y + \frac{Y}{4}\right) \qquad \textit{Q.e.d.}$$

The proof that the constants Q and S, computed for common years, also apply to the latter part of a *leap* year (after the intercalary day), and that the DN found by these two formulas, requires a correction of (+1) for the first part of a leap year (to and including the intercalary day), is deferred to *Section 33*.

In finding Easter, both formulas are applied as given above, because for this purpose the *second* DL, current after the intercalary day in leap years, must be used, since Easter is always later than Feb 29.

The polynomials $\left(6\,H + Y + \frac{Y}{4}\right)$ and $\left(5\,H + \frac{H}{4} + Y + \frac{Y}{4}\right)$ should be noted because they are of frequent application.

Use of Table I to find dominical letters

This new table gives the DL for any year of the Christian Era with a minimum of effort, and is used as follows:

Divide the number of the given year by 28; increase the remainder (R) by the term (T) proper to the period, and with the argument (R + T) enter the second part of the table to find the required DL. In NS century years that are not exact multiples of 400, the *first* of the two letters thus found is current throughout the entire year.

Subtract 28 from (R + T) whenever possible.

Examples: Find the dominical letters for the same years as above.

(1)	AD 1451	We have: 1451 ÷ 28	leaves	R = 23,	T = 0	DL is C
(2)	AD 1452	1452 ÷ 28	"	R = 24,	T = 0	DL is BA
(3)	AD 0	0 ÷ 28	"	R = 0,	T = 0	DL is DC
(4)	AD 1935	1935 ÷ 28	"	R = 3,	T = 12	DL is F
(5)	AD 1936	1936 ÷ 28	"	R = 4,	T = 12	DL is ED
(6)	AD 3170	3170 ÷ 28	"	R = 6,	T = 16	DL is D
(7)	AD 3700 (common year)	3700 ÷ 28	"	R = 4,	T = 8	DL is C (only).
(8)	AD 1582 to Oct. 4	1582 ÷ 28	"	R = 14,	T = 0	DL is G
	AD 1582 from Oct. 15,	1582 ÷ 28	"	R = 14,	T = 20, (R + T) = 6	DL is C

Construction of Table I

The dominical letters of the first (4 × 7) or 28 years of the Christian Era form a repeating series, shown here in Table M, together with a part of the following series; they were computed by means of Formula I.

TABLE M

R	DL
0	DC
1	B
2	A
3	G
4	FE
5	D
6	C
7	B
8	AG
9	F
10	E
11	D
12	CB
13	A
14	G
15	F
16	ED
17	C
18	B
19	A
20	GF
21	E
22	D
23	C
24	BA
25	G
26	F
27	E
28	DC
29	B
30	A
31	G
32	FE
33	D
34	C
35	B
36	AG

So long, therefore, as *every* fourth year is a leap year, that is, from AD 0 to Oct 4, 1582, the dominical letter of any given year can be found by dividing the number of that year by 28; for with the remainder (R) as argument, Table M will give the year's dominical letters.

But what will happen, if one of these leap years is reduced to a common year, with the condition that the *first* of its two dominical letters shall be current throughout the entire year?

For instance, let it be assumed that the leap year AD 4 were to be so reduced by the omission of its intercalary day; F would then be its dominical letter for the entire common year 4. (Table M.) In the next year, AD 5, the DL would have to be E, followed by D, C, BA, etc. This sequence of letters: E, D, C, BA, begins in Table M at R = 21. Hence, this table might still be retained provided that for the year 5 and every following year, the remainder R were augmented by (21 − 5) or 16 years, giving (R + 16) as argument.

Likewise, if another leap year later on were reduced to a common year, Table M might still be retained if 16 years were again added, making (R + 32) the argument, or (R + 4) after 28 is subtracted; and so forth.

Now let us see what happened in AD 1582.

TABLE N

Years	DL
1580	CB
1581	A
1582 to Oct 4	G
1582 from Oct 15	C
1583	B
1584	AG

The dominical letters in Table N have been computed by means of Formula I and Formula II.

The sequence of letters: CB, A, G, ends, in Table M, at R = 14; the sequence C, B, AG, begins at R = 34. Hence, one may continue to use Table M after Oct 15, 1582, provided that the remainder R is augmented by (34 − 14) or 20, giving as argument (R + 20).

After AD 1700, the first of the century leap years to be reduced to a common year, the augmentum to the remainder R becomes (20 + 16) or 8, after subtracting 28; after 1800, it becomes (8 + 16) or 24; after 1900, it becomes (24 + 16) or 12.

The year 2000 is a leap year and the augmentum remains unchanged at 12; after 2100 it becomes (12 + 16) or 0; and so forth.

The construction of Table I is now plain. The term (T), additive to R, is listed at the left of the Table according to the period containing the given year; at the right is a copy of Table M, with (R + T) as argument to determine the required dominical letter.

Section 4

The Julian solar calendar. Its reform in 1582. The Gregorian Rule. Reason for this rule.

A *solar calendar* measures and records time by means of years and days. These are incommensurable quantities, having no common measure. Subordinate units of solar time are the unequal months and the weeks.

A revision of the ancient Roman calendar was undertaken with the authorization of Julius Caesar in 44 BC by Sosigenes, a Greek mathematician. He based his solar calendar on a mean tropical year of 365.25 days. As this value was somewhat too large, his calendar advanced relatively to the seasons at the rate of about three days every four centuries. In other words, spring began three days earlier by his calendar than it had begun four centuries before. By the sixteenth century, this discrepancy between the Julian solar calendar and the seasons of the year had become quite marked, spring beginning about Mar 12 by the calendar instead of Mar 21, thereby interfering with the proper celebration of Easter, which was based, as we shall see, on the calendar date Mar 21.

A reform of the Julian solar calendar was therefore undertaken by Pope Gregory XIII, in AD 1582.

The Gregorian corrections to the solar calendar comprised:

1° The omission of ten dates from the calendar, Thursday, Oct 4, 1582, being immediately followed by Friday, Oct 15; this restored the calendar date Mar 21 to the approximate position that it had held relative to the beginning of spring in AD 325, the year of the Council of Nicaea.

2° The substitution of Jan 1 as the beginning of the calendar year, instead of Mar 1, or other calendar date previously used.

3° The adoption of a simple expedient to prevent a recurrence of such a discrepancy; it may be stated in the following rule.

Gregorian Rule: Hereafter a year whose number in the Christian Era is exactly divisible by four shall be a leap year; but a century year shall be a common year, unless it is an exact multiple of 400.

The years AD 1600, 2000, 2400, etc., are therefore leap years, while the years AD 1700, 1800, 1900, 2100, etc., though multiples of four, are common years.

To understand the reason for this Gregorian Rule, we take as epoch the beginning of the Christian Era, AD 0, in order that the fourth year thereafter may be AD 4, the one-hundredth year, AD 100, etc.; and we shall again assume, as in *Section 3*, that the Gregorian Rule was in force from the beginning of the Era; and for the mean tropical year we take the value adopted in 1582:

365 days, 5 hours, 49 minutes, 12 seconds

or the Gregorian mean tropical year = 365.2425 days.

Then we have:

At the beginning of AD 1 the correction needed by the calendar, because of the preceding year, was	+0.2425 days
At the beginning of AD 4 the correction needed by the calendar was + 0.2425 × 4, or	+0.97 days
This year was *increased* by one whole day, making it a leap year, and the correction then needed was	−0.03 days
At the beginning of AD 100 the correction was −0.03 × 25, or	−0.75 days
If we assume that this first year of the century was at once *diminished* by one whole day, and reduced to a common year, the correction to the calendar became	+0.25 days
By AD 400 the correction needed was +0.25 × 4, or	+1.00 days

Had this century year been *increased* by one whole day and thereby restored as a leap year, there would have been no further correction needed, and the process could have begun anew.

The period of 400 years in the Gregorian Calendar is, therefore, an *exact repeating unit* of solar time.

Christopher Clavius, S.J., one of the principal authors of the reform, was so confident of the adopted length of the mean solar year that he computed a table* to AD 300,000, in which *every* exact multiple of 400 was listed as a leap year. We shall see in *Section 24* that such is not the case. Beginning with AD 1600, every thirty-two-hundredth year thereafter must be a common year. His table, therefore, becomes inaccurate with the year 4800. Unless

* See his classical work: *Romani Calendarii a Gregorio XIII P. M. Restituti Explicatio.*

corrected, the error will cause the calendar date Mar 21 again to advance relatively to the beginning of spring at the rate of one day every 3200 years.

Section 5

The Inherent Imperfection of every solar calendar

Table II shows the corrections needed by the Gregorian yearly calendar at the beginning of March of every year during the 400-year cycle. The computation is based on a Gregorian tropical year of 365.2425 days; 0.2425 of a day is added every year and one whole day, corresponding to February 29, is subtracted in every leap year. The results are tabulated to two decimals. The century years, 100, 200, and 300 are common years. The cycle begins with AD 1600, 2000, 2400, etc. It is seen from the table that the corrections reach their minimum value (m) of -0.72 of a day in the year 96, and their maximum value (M) of $+1.47$ days in the year 303 of the cycle.

This table illustrates the inherent imperfection of *every* solar calendar; for a calendar can keep abreast of the continuous march of time only by the occasional application of a whole corrective day at fixed intervals, usually resulting in an over-correction. These over-corrections, in turn, accumulate and require the application of a corrective day contrary to the former, and so forth.

The following consideration will help one to realize the relation between the sun, the yearly calendar, and the mean vernal equinox.

Our standard indicator of time is the sun. To an observer on the earth the sun seems to revolve around the earth westward once every twenty-four hours; but superimposed on this apparent diurnal motion is an apparent eastward motion of the sun, through the sky, completing one revolution about the earth in 365.2425 days, or in one Gregorian tropical year. To simplify matters, let it be assumed that this apparent annual motion of the sun takes place along the circumference of a circle which has the earth as center and a radius of roughly 92 million miles. Let this circle—the sun's apparent path—lie in the plane of the ecliptic, and let the sun move uniformly along this path, covering equal arcs in equal periods of time. This is near enough to the true conditions for our purpose.

This sun, as viewed from the earth, is projected against its background, the ecliptic, a great circle of the celestial sphere, and describes on the ecliptic a continuous record of its annual motion. This record, however, is not a yearly calendar, because it is a record of this one year only; the next year's record will be a different one. The essential element of a yearly calendar is that it shall be the same for every year. To obtain this we conceive the ecliptic itself, or better, a huge ring coinciding with the ecliptic, as graduated into 365 equal parts, corresponding to the number of whole days in a common year. This graduated calendar ring* is conceived as movable within narrow limits along the ecliptic against the stationary vernal equinox.

This vernal equinox is not the true equinox, or the point on the ecliptic where the projection of the real sun crosses the plane of the equator at the beginning of spring, but the mean equinox, thus called because it occupies an average or mean position within the range of the true equinox. One may here disregard the annual precession westward of the mean equinox, because the tropical year makes allowance for it, and the calendar ring has thereby been made to share, generally speaking, in that precession.

In the figure on page 14, let the outer circle represent the ecliptic† or the yearly calendar ring, and let the inner circle represent the apparent path of the sun (☉) with the earth (⊕) at its center; let the point in the sun's path between the earth and the mean vernal equinox be marked by the symbol for the latter (♈), and let all be viewed from the north pole of the ecliptic.

In the initial position let the sun coincide with the equinox and let the point of the calendar ring, Mar 21.00, be opposite both. After one year the sun will again come around to the equinox; but the calendar point Mar 21.2425 (not Mar 21.00), will now be opposite the equinox. The imperfect calendar, being graduated for whole days only, and having omitted a fractional part of a day (0.2425), has gradually moved clockwise by that amount against the stationary equinox. After a second year the dislocation will be doubled and Mar 21.4850 will be opposite the equinox; after the third year it will be Mar 21.7275, and after the fourth year it would be Mar 21.9700; but an extra date, February 29, has been put into the calendar during this year causing the calendar to snap back counterclockwise one whole day. The result is that Mar 21.00 now stands 0.03 of a day to the left of the equinox.

This over-correction of 0.03 of a day every four years shows what will happen in the long run if *every* fourth year is to be a leap year. These over-corrections will accumulate and after (100 × 4) or 400 years they will amount to (100 × 0.03), or three days, and the calendar point Mar 21.00 will stand three days to the left of the equinox. After another 400 years it will be six days, after another 400 years, nine days, etc. This is precisely

* A wall calendar is merely a reproduction, conveniently separated into monthly sections, of this imaginary calendar ring along the ecliptic. On any large-sized globe similar calendar graduations are found on the ecliptic circle to indicate roughly the angular distance of the sun from the vernal equinox (its celestial longitude) on any day of the calendar year.

† The figure represents the ecliptic, a great circle of the celestial sphere, as of finite dimensions, and the equinox as a point on the sun's path; this is unobjectionable when, not linear distances, but only angular distances are to be illustrated.

what happened to the Julian Calendar; in Mar, 1500, not Mar 21.00 but Mar 12.00 stood opposite the equinox. One frequently reads the statement that in the Julian Calendar the equinox retrograded three days every four centuries; it would be more correct to say that the calendar point Mar 21.00, and with it the whole solar calendar shifted its position counterclockwise against the equinox by that amount.

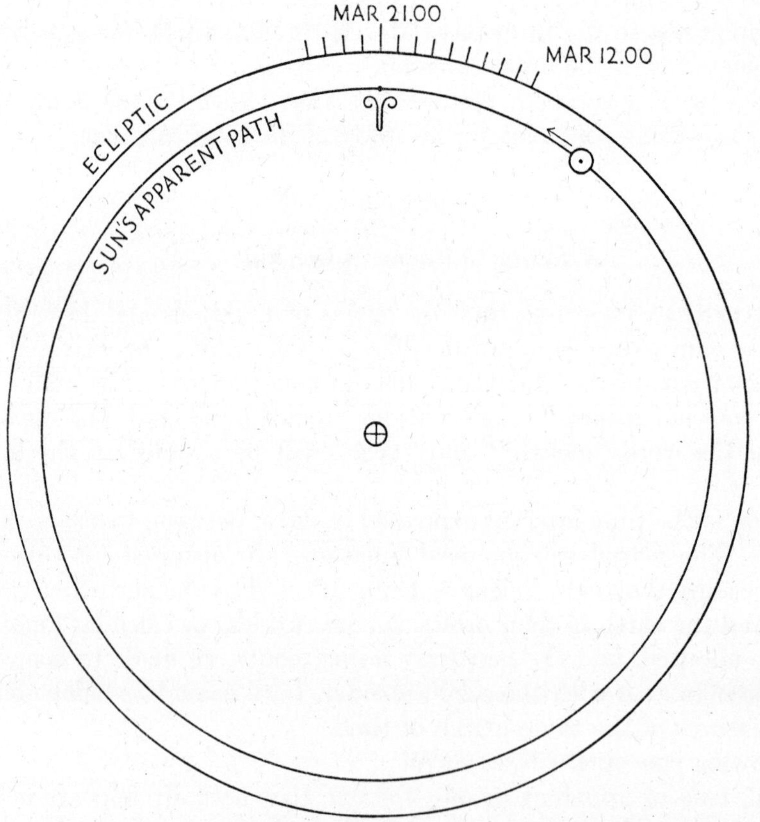

Figure illustrating the relation between the sun, the yearly calendar and the mean vernal equinox.

In the Gregorian solar calendar the omission of the intercalary date (February 29) in every century year not divisible by 400 over-corrects the calendar in the opposite direction, and the retention of the intercalary day in the 400th year brings the calendar back to the initial position, with the calendar point Mar 21.00 again opposite the equinox.

One should familiarize himself with the fact that it is not the mean equinox that moves relatively to Mar 21, but the calendar point Mar 21.00;

and with this point the whole yearly calendar, due to its own imperfections swings to and fro about the equinox. The total range of that swing during the 400-year period is shown by Table II to be (0.72 + 1.48) or 2.2 days, with the result that the vernal equinox can fall on March 20, 21, or 22 by the calendar. There is no possible way to remedy this awkward fact; it is an inherent defect in the structure of *any* solar calendar, and the Gregorian Calendar should not be singled out for criticism on that account. We shall see in *Section 18* that the application of an extra corrective day in 1582 limited the equinox to the three days March 19, 20, and 21, for a practical reason connected with the lunar calendar.

Familiarity with a concrete picture, like that shown in the figure, will save much tantalizing confusion in the study of the solar calendar.

Section 6

A Lunar Calendar in General

A LUNAR CALENDAR measures time by means of lunations and days; these are again incommensurable quantities like the solar units, the year and the day. The lunar part of the Christian Calendar measures time, but unlike the solar part, does not record it; the lunations are not numbered. For the sake of clearness the word "month"* and "year" will be avoided in the lunar calendar.

A lunation is the time interval expressed in days, between two successive new moons. The actual astronomical lunations are unsuited for calendar purposes, because they vary in length, being affected by the perturbations of the moon and the earth in their orbits. A conventional or calendar lunation is therefore adopted, and the necessary adjustments are made to keep the lunar calendar in step with the solar calendar, both calendars being simultaneous measures of the same march of time.

The following concepts will be useful:

1° The real, true or apparent moon—the one that actually appears in the sky—revolves about the earth conterclockwise as seen from the north pole of the heavens, eastward as seen from the earth, with a motion that is continuous but not uniform; its motion about the earth is at times accelerated, at times retarded, due principally to the fact that its orbit is an ellipse. The period of its revolution, the apparent lunation, will therefore vary in length.

* The month was originally a lunar unit of time, and in the Hebrew and the Mohammedan Calendars it is still the equivalent of the lunation. But in the Julian and the Gregorian Calendars, the months have lost all relation to the lunations and are now subordinate units of the solar year.

2° The mean moon is an imaginary one, conceived as revolving about the earth with a continuous and uniform motion, such that its mean lunation of 29.53 days will be the average of a sufficiently large number of revolutions of the apparent moon.

3° The calendar moon is an imaginary one that revolves about the earth with a discontinuous motion, advancing by whole days only—just as the minute-hand of a wall clock that is driven by a central master clock advances by whole minutes.

As viewed from the earth, the mean moon is at times east of the apparent moon, at times west of it; for practical reasons the lunar calendar has been adjusted in such a way that the calendar moon either coincides with the mean moon, or lags behind it (west of it) by as much as two days.

The Church's calendar is both solar and lunar. Were it not for the computation of Easter and the movable feasts depending thereon, a lunar calendar would be unnecessary. The details of the Gregorian reform of the traditional lunar calendar are given in *Section 18* and *Section 19*.

The reform of the lunar calendar in 1582 was due principally to Aloysius Lilius,* a physician of Perugia, as the reform of the solar calendar was principally the work of Clavius,* though on both calendars there had been many learned papers submitted in previous years, beginning with the thirteenth century. To Clavius was entrusted the task of verifying the computations and of defending the completed calendar reform.

SECTION 7

The Easter Controversy. Quartodecimans. Easter defined.

THE RESURRECTION occurred on the first day of the week (Sunday) after the Crucifixion, and after the Jewish feast of Passover. (John 18–20.) The Passover was ordered in the Old Law to be observed "on the fourteenth day of the first month" (Leviticus 23:5), and that was the first month (Nisan) of the old Hebrew year whose fourteenth day (or full moon) occurred at, or next after, the beginning of spring. Since the Council of Nicaea (AD 325) the calendar date Mar 21 has been the calendar equinox for the Christian world.

For many centuries the Hebrews determined the new moon dates, monthly festivals of theirs, by observation, when the thin sickle of the nascent moon first became distinguishable; later on they adopted a system of computation, and that is their practice at the present time. The Hebrew calendar day begins soon after sundown of the preceding evening.

The proper date for the celebration of Easter was a much disputed ques-

* See *Catholic Encyclopedia, s. v.*

tion in the early Christian Church. Some of the Orientals celebrated Easter on the fourteenth day itself, whence they were called Quartodecimans; Easter thus usually fell on a week day, like Passover. In the Christian world generally, Easter was celebrated on the first Sunday after the fourteenth moon. As early as AD 190, Pope St. Victor had excommunicated some groups in Asia Minor as Quartodecimans, for in that year St. Irenaeus, Bishop of Lyons, himself an oriental by birth, wrote to Rome to intercede for them.* The Council of Nicaea decided the question against the Quartodecimans and prescribed uniformity.

Easter, therefore, must be defined as the first Sunday *after* the fourteenth moon that occurs on or after Mar 21. It is so intimately connected with this calendar date, that if Mar 21 wanders from its proper place relative to the seasons of the year, Easter will follow it in its aberration. That is what gradually took place in the Julian Calendar (*Section 4*); hence the Gregorian Reform was occasioned by a liturgical necessity, and at the request of the Council of Trent.

In determining Easter it must be noted that, *not* the real or apparent moon, nor yet a mean or average moon, but a conventional or calendar moon is used; *not* the true astronomical equinox, nor yet the mean astronomical equinox, but a conventional or calendar equinox, namely Mar 21, is used to determine the date of Easter.

In the Roman Church the Easter date was originally determined by means of a $(4 \times 28 - 28)$ or 84-year cycle,† probably brought to Rome in subapostolic times from the Roman Province of Asia, that had been under St. John's jurisdiction. Since in the Julian Calendar *every* fourth year was a leap year, this cycle yielded a repeating series of dominical letters, but the Easter dates derived by their means did not form a perfect repeating series, even from one cycle to the next.

It was this defective paschal cycle that was received from Rome by the Celts at their conversion to Christianity, and was retained by the Celtic monks and missioners long after Rome had changed to a new cycle, thus giving rise to an Easter controversy in the West, differing from that with the Quatrodecimans of the East. This controversy, as far as Saxon England was concerned, was settled at the Synod of Whitby‡ in AD 664.

At the suggestion of Dionysus Exiguus, the simple 19-year cycle of Meton was introduced at Rome; it had long been used at Constantinople and in the East, where Greek influence predominated.

The determination of the Easter date is, of course, a matter for the Catholic Church to decide, since Easter is *her* feast of the Resurrection.

* See *Catholic Encyclopedia,* Vol. VIII, p. 130.

† See *Catholic Encyclopedia,* Vol. VI, p. 360.

‡ *Ibid., s.v.*

She has the authority to prescribe its celebration on any calendar date that she deems proper. Those Quatrodecimans who refused to conform to the Easter practice of the universal Church were regarded, not merely as schismatics, but as probable heretics, because of their erroneous view that the Levitical ceremonial law of the Passover (Leviticus 23:5) binds the Christian world. To be consistent, they should have kept the Jewish Sabbath instead of the Christian Sunday.

In determining her Easter date, the Church has regard to the Jews' computation of their Passover date and tries to avoid having Easter coincide with, or precede Passover. Her motive is not animosity towards the Jews, but the apparent anomaly of having the Resurrection, which occurred after the Crucifixion, celebrated before, or on the same day as the slaying of the paschal lamb (Passover), which was a prophetic figure of the Crucifixion.

In neither attempt is she entirely successful. Thus, in five years* of the twentieth century Easter coincides with Passover; and in a period of 228 years, from 1845 to 2072, Easter precedes Passover 36 times, when the Jews put their Passover one whole lunation later than the Christian calendar would require.

SECTION 8

The Metonic cycle, solar and lunar. Thirty kinds of lunar cycle.

Meton, a Greek (*c.* BC 432) discovered that a new moon usually takes place on the same date on which one occurred nineteen years before, and that 235 lunations intervened.

Therefore, 19 years = 235 lunations.

This fact affords two yardsticks for measuring time; a *solar* cycle of 19 years, and a *lunar* cycle of 235 lunations.

The Christian luni-solar calendar uses both yardsticks. They may be compared as follows:

Solar 19-year Cycle		Lunar 235-lunation Cycle	
365	days (common year)	29.5	days (approximate lunation)
×19		×235	
6935		6932.5	
+4.75	($\frac{19}{4}$ intercalary days)	+4.75	($\frac{19}{4}$ intercalary days)
		+2.5	(required by Meton's discovery)
6939.75		6939.75	

* In 1903, 1923, 1927, 1954, 1981, The First of Tishri falls on Tuesday, and Passover, 163 days earlier, occurs on Sunday; in these five years it is Easter Sunday. See Woolhouse, *Measures, Weights, and Monies of all Nations*. See also Table in *Encyclopedia Britannica, s. v.* "Calendar."

Both yardsticks are of constant length; and they contain the intercalary day in *every* fourth year as an essential part.

Those $2\frac{1}{2}$ days of the lunar cycle, required by Meton's discovery, are distributed among the 235 approximate lunations of $29\frac{1}{2}$ days each, by giving seven of them an additional half-day each, making thirty-day lunations of them, and by deducting one whole day at, or near the end of the cycle. To avoid decimals, the remaining 228 lunations are taken alternately as of 29 and 30 days each; namely, 114 of 29 days and 114 of 30 days. These adjustments modify the approximate lunation of $29\frac{1}{2}$ days assumed above.

The conditions for these adjustments in the 235-lunation cycle are:

1° The length of the cycle (6939.75 days) must not be altered, for it is one of our yardsticks for the measurement of time.

2° Every cycle must be a repeating one.

3° Every cycle must contain, though not in succession, twelve new moons to the solar year twelve times, and thirteen new moons to the solar year seven times, because

$$235 = 12 \times 12 + 7 \times 13$$

where $$12 + 7 = 19$$

4° The cycle must contain no duplicate new moon dates, because it is used in constructing the yearly calendar.

5° Every Dec–Jan lunation must contain thirty days, because the determination of the first new moon date in every year depends on it. But the last lunation of the cycle usually contains only twenty nine days to satisfy condition 2°.

These conditions are all possible of simultaneous fulfilment. They will become clearer as we proceed.

There are thirty possible kinds of this 235-lunation cycle, depending on the first new moon date of the cycle; all are of the same length, but of *different structure*, due to the initial new moon date and to the various positions assigned to the adjustments in each.

Apparently every lunar cycle contains only 6935 days, being constructed on the basis of nineteen common years; in *reality*, each cycle contains 6939.75 days. This will become clear when it is shown, in *Section 21*, how the intercalary days of the leap years are allowed for, without interfering with either yardstick.

One such lunar cycle is shown in Table V; it was used during the period 1582 to 1699.

Another lunar cycle is shown in Table VI, in use during the present period 1900 to 2199.

A third lunar cycle is shown in Table XII; it was used from BC 44 to AD 1582.

SECTION 9

The Epacts derived and defined. The Solar Equation.

WE NOW APPROACH a difficult part of our subject: the theory and use of epacts.

Let it be proposed to find nineteen numbers that will give in succession the age of the calendar moon at the beginning of every year of a given 235-lunation cycle, all years being regarded for the present as common years. The following fact points the way.

A solar common year exceeds twelve lunations of $29\frac{1}{2}$ days each by eleven days, since

$$365 = 12 \times 29\tfrac{1}{2} + 11.$$

This means that the calendar moon will be eleven days older at the end of any given common year than it was at the beginning.

To apply this fact to our purpose, let it be assumed that the first year of the cycle began at midnight with the moon *one* day old, the preceding day, Dec 31, having been a new moon day. Table V will illustrate this case.

The second year will begin with the moon (1 + 11) or 12 days old.

The third year will begin with the moon (12 + 11) or 23 days old, and it would end with an excess of (23 + 11) or 34 days. Now, thirty of these days are applied to the third year as an additional completed lunation—the first of the so-called "embolismic" lunations, from ἐμβάλλειν, meaning *to intercalate.**

The fourth year will therefore begin with the moon (34 − 30) or four days old, and the fifth year with the moon 15 days old.

The sixth year will begin with the moon 26 days old, and it would end with an excess of 37 days. Again 30 of these days are applied to the sixth year as an additional completed lunation—the second embolismic lunation—so that the seventh year will begin with the moon 7 days old, and so forth.

The nineteenth year, the last of the cycle, will begin with the moon 19 days old, and it would end with an excess of (19 + 11) or 30 days. However, that the number-series may be a repeating one, twelve days (instead of eleven) are added and the last year ends with (19 + 12) or 31 days. Thirty of these days are applied to the nineteenth year of the cycle as an additional

* In the 235-lunation cycle, the adjustments mentioned in *Section 8* may reduce some of these 30-day embolismic lunations to 29-day lunations. See Table V, years whose golden numbers are 6, 9, 17, and 19.

completed lunation—the seventh and last of the embolismic lunations in this cycle—and the next year begins with the moon again one day old as nineteen years before.

This addition of an extra unit after every nineteenth year of whatever cycle is in use, is not arbitrary; the sum of the additions must equal the sum of the subtractions.

Hence $$19 \times 11 + 1 = 7 \times 30$$

As a consequence, the series of nineteen numbers, like the 235-lunation cycle itself, is a repeating series

for $$E + (19 \times 11 + 1) - (7 \times 30) = E$$

where E is the age of the moon at the beginning of the cycle.

The nineteen numbers thus found are called *epacts*, from *ἐπακταὶ ἡμέραι*, meaning additional days, superfluous days, left-over days, or simply "the excess."

So, to find the nineteen epacts of any 235-lunation cycle, the rule is: Begin with the age of the moon at the beginning of the first year of the cycle; add eleven days every following year, but twelve days after the last year of the series; drop thirty days whenever possible.*

The epact of a given year, therefore, may be defined as:

1° The excess after the last completed lunation of the preceding year to the end of that year (with the exception given in the footnote).

2° The age of the moon at the beginning of the given year (midnight).

The series of epacts found above

1, 12, 23, 4, 15, 26, 7, 18, 29, 10, 21, 2, 13, 24, 5, 16, 27, 8, 19,

corresponding to the golden numbers 1 to 19 (from which they are usually distinguished by the use of Roman Notation), was in use from Oct 15, 1582 to 1699 (incl.). See Table V.

In 1700, the first century year that was a common year, the intercalary date was not added to the solar calendar, thus augmenting all succeeding solar dates by one day; for instance, what would have been Feb 29 in the civil calendar, became Mar 1, etc.

* Thirty days cannot be dropped unless at least one day is left over with which to start the next year, since there is no zero-epact. Hence, if by addition of the eleven or twelve days to the epact, exactly thirty results, this number 30 is not dropped, but is represented by an asterisk (✳) and carried forward into the next year, at the end of which it is dropped, leaving the epact XI for the following year. See Table VI, lines whose golden numbers are: 11, 12, 13. The lunar cycle, too, shows that the year 11 had no embolismic lunation.

The epact ✳ means that the year begins with a completed lunation of thirty days, that could not be dropped for the reason just given.

This automatically required the succeeding new moon dates, since they are expressed in solar time, to be all likewise increased by one day; this increase was effected by *subtracting* one day from what would have been the epact X for 1700, line X of Table VIII being replaced by line IX. That, of course, required a like reduction of all the other epacts of the series previously used, and gave rise to the following new series of epacts, applicable to the period 1700 to 1899 (incl.).

*, 11, 22, 3, 14, 25, 6, 17, 28, 9, 20, 1, 12, 23, 4, 15, 26, 7, 18.

In like manner, in every century year not divisible by 400, a similar correction of minus one day must be applied to the epacts, ordinarily giving rise to a new series of epacts; this negative correction is called the "*Solar Equation.*"* See Table III and Table IV.

Section 10

Inaccuracy of Meton's Lunar Cycle. The Lunar Equation.

It was assumed above (*Section 8*) that the lunar cycle of 235 lunations was exactly equal to 19 solar years. As a matter of fact it was taken too large. For this reason, a *positive* correction, as we shall see, must occasionally be applied to the epacts.

This excess of the lunar cycle over its correct value may be computed by the use of the mean astronomical lunation:

29 days, 12 hours, 44 minutes, 2.8 seconds,

or A mean lunation = 29.530588 days.

We have:

The lunar cycle adopted in *Section 8*	6939.75000 days
The true lunar cycle (235 × 29.530588)	6939.68818 days
The correction to the epacts every 19 years is	+0.06182 days

This amounts to one whole day in $\frac{19}{0.06182}$ or $307\frac{1}{3}$ years.

In order to make the corrections to the lunar calendar applicable in

* The word "equation" is frequently used in mathematics to designate a *single* quantity, the application of which serves to equate two other quantities (to make them equal to one another). Thus, in the two series of epacts given above, the application of (−1) to any epact of the first series equates it to the corresponding epact of the second series. For instance, in the case of the last epact of each series one may write:

$$19 - 1 = 18$$

This (−1), though belonging to the lunar calendar, originates in the solar calendar (from the omission of the intercalary day), and is therefore called the "*Solar* Equation."

century years, the calendar reformers in 1582 adopted a correction of plus one day every $312\frac{1}{2}$ years. Since

$$8 \times 312\tfrac{1}{2} = 2500,$$

they decided to add one corrective day, the so-called *"Lunar Equation,"* to the epacts every 300 years seven times in succession, and one day after the next 400 years, because

$$7 \times 300 + 400 = 2500.$$

This process, beginning with the addition of one day in AD 1800,* as the last of a preceding series of eight such corrections, is to continue indefinitely to keep the two yardsticks, the solar and the lunar, abreast of one another, and thus to maintain the two calendars, the solar and the lunar, in step over a very long period of time. But see *Section 25.*

One such corrective day, owing to the excess of the lunar cycle over its correct value, is due in AD 2400. Directly this correction will require the *subtraction* of one day from the following new moon dates of the lunar cycle till then in use; but this subtraction will be effected by the *addition* of one day to each of its epacts. What would have been the epact III for AD 2400 will become IV, thus automatically diminishing all following new moon dates by one day (see Table VIII, lines III and IV), and giving rise to a new series of epacts beginning with AD 2400.

This process is therefore equivalent to *setting back* the invariable lunar yardstick one day, to diminish its new moon dates by that amount, leaving the solar yardstick unaffected; for this correction is due solely to the excess of the lunar cycle (6939.75 days), over its correct value.

One can avoid confusion as to the working of solar and lunar equations by remembering that the epacts in the yearly calendar (Table IX) stand in *inverse* order to the calendar dates. Hence,

1° A solar equation diminishes the epacts and augments the new moon dates.

2° A lunar equation augments the epacts and diminishes the new moon dates.

To visualize the application of the two yardsticks to the measurement of time, it may be helpful in this somewhat abstruse matter, to use the following comparison.†

* More accurate results would be obtained if the lunar equations due in 1800, 2400, 4300, etc., were each applied one century earlier; but this would destroy the simplicity of the rule stated above.

† This image is the perfect counterpart of the reality, save that the markings of a lunar strip will indicate *mean,* instead of calendar new moon dates.

Imagine an indefinitely long vertical strip of paper, accurately ruled; its spaces will represent day by day the march of time which, of course, never varies.

Picture three measuring strips of transparent tape:

1° The first strip is 6939.75 spaces long and un-ruled; this will be the solar yardstick.

2° The second strip is of the same length, but accurately divided into 235 equal parts; this will be the *traditional* lunar yardstick.

3° The third strip is only 6939.68818 spaces long, and accurately divided into 235 equal parts; this will be the *correct* lunar yardstick. Its divisions will be slightly *shorter* than those of the preceding strip.

First apply the traditional lunar strip to the ruled paper; its markings will indicate thereon the new moon days; they are as yet undated.

Next replace the lunar strip by the transparent solar strip, and on the lines that show through, write the calendar dates, month by month and day by day, to be erased and re-written every nineteen years, when the solar strip is re-applied to the ruled paper. Every fourth year must have its intercalary day, which is an essential part of both yardsticks. (*Section 8.*)

Then superimpose the traditional lunar strip on the solar strip and ruled paper. Both strips being equally long and transparent, the graduation marks of the lunar strip will indicate both the new moon days of that cycle on the ruled paper, and their calendar dates on the solar strip.

Time and again every nineteen years the combined measures are thus applied to the ruled paper. All goes well until the time arrives when an intercalary date (Feb 29) must be omitted on the solar strip. The very next new moon which, of course, occurs according to schedule, finds the new moon day called, for instance, Mar 2 instead of Mar 1. But the lunar cycle hitherto used calls for a new moon on the calendar date Mar 1. All following new moon dates of the lunar cycle must therefore be increased by one day to make them agree with the altered solar calendar. This is effected by applying the solar equation to the epacts.

Finally, place both lunar strips side by side over the ruled paper and the solar strip; it will be seen how the graduation marks of the traditional lunar strip, like the markings of a vernier, tend to outrun those of the correct lunar strip. After 307 years, or 16 applications of the three strips to the ruled paper, a mark of the traditional strip will have gained one whole space of the ruled paper over the correct strip and will indicate on the ruled paper below a new moon day that is one day ahead of the correct new moon day. This requires that the traditional lunar strip be set back one day, thereby reducing by one day all the new moon dates that its graduation marks indicate on the ruled paper below. This reduction of new moon dates is effected by applying the lunar equation to the epacts.

Both kinds of corrections, the solar and the lunar equations, are shown in Table III, with their effects on the epacts. This table begins with a purely *theoretical* part, showing the conditions that would have prevailed, had the Gregorian luni-solar calendar been in use from the beginning of the Christian Era; in that case, of course, no reform would have been needed in 1582.

In the years 1800, 2100, 2700, etc., no change in the current series of epacts is required, because the lunar and solar equations applicable in each of those years neutralize one another, since they are of opposite algebraic signs.

With the aid of Table III, Table IV is constructed containing successive series of epacts and the period, within which each series is applicable. These are *reformed* epacts; in this table the traditional series of Old Style epacts of Table XII

XI, XXII, III, XIV, etc.

does not appear before AD 6200. See *Section 18.*

SECTION 11

Construction of the New Style yearly calendar.

IN WHAT FOLLOWS, for the sake of brevity, the words "new moon" and "lunation" will always be understood to mean calendar or conventional new moons and lunations, not astronomical or true ones.

The construction of the reformed yearly calendar is based on the important fact that 30 common years exceed 371 lunations of $29\frac{1}{2}$ days each by $5\frac{1}{2}$ days, or 11 half-days.

$$30 \times 365 = 371 \times 29\tfrac{1}{2} + 5\tfrac{1}{2}$$

A beginning is made with the epact ✻ (meaning 30) and the new moon date Jan 1, and a 30-year cycle of 371 lunations is constructed (Table VII) on the assumption that all years are common years; how the intervening leap years are treated will be shown in *Section 21.*

In order to make the 371 lunations *exactly* equal to 30 common years, the 11 half-days are added to 11 such lunations, making them 30-day lunations. To avoid decimals, the remaining 360 lunations are taken alternately as of 29 and 30 days each, that is, 180 of 29 days, and 180 of 30 days, thus averaging $29\frac{1}{2}$ days each.

The conditions for the distribution of the 11 half-days are:

1° The Dec–Jan lunation must always contain 30 days; this is necessary in order that later on, at the beginning of any year, the epact may always be subtracted from the *same* number 30 (never from 29) to give the number of days still remaining to the end of that lunation. As a consequence, a given year's epact plus its first new moon date will always equal 31 days.

2° *Only* six (371 – 365) pairs of new moon dates may consist of identical dates, in order that one of every pair may be omitted, leaving *365* different new moon dates—one for every day of the common year—thus making a yearly calendar possible. Every year of new moon dates in Table VII is preceded by its epact. These thirty epacts are computed by the annual addition of 11 days *without exception*, and the subtraction of 30 days whenever possible. This subtraction of 30 will occur eleven times because the 30-year cycle contains eleven years with 13 new moons each, and nineteen years with 12 new moons each,

since $$371 = 11 \times 13 + 19 \times 12$$

where $$11 + 19 = 30$$

The epact series is therefore a repeating one, because

$$* + (30 \times 11) - (11 + 30) = *$$

In fulfilling condition 1° the corrective half-days would normally be added at the end of the year. However, in the six years whose epacts are *, XXIX, XXVIII, XXVII, XXVI, and XXV, for practical reasons the corrective half-day is shifted from the end of the year to near the beginning, in order to make the first complete lunation in each of these six years a 30-day lunation. Despite this shift, the Dec–Jan lunation at the end of the year will still be a 30-day lunation as required by condition 1°.

The lines of this Table VII are next *re-arranged* in the order of diminishing epacts, which is the same as the calendar order of the first new moon dates of the single lines. This has been done in Table VIII; to our surprise it is at once apparent that condition 2° has already been fulfilled by the shift of the corrective half-day in line XXV. All the new moon dates of this table are different, except only the six pairs of identical dates on lines XXV and XXIV, namely: Feb 5, Apr 5, Jun 3, Aug 1, Sep 29 and Nov 27.

These six new moon dates are now omitted from line XXV; they will not be missed because each stands above an identical date on line XXIV.

To return to Table VII. On the omission of the six new moon dates with their lunations in line XXV, the 371-new moon cycle becomes a 365-new moon cycle, and it is a repeating cycle because its last new moon on Dec 2, on the addition of 30 days is followed by the next new moon on Jan 1, with which condition the cycle began.

The 30 possible kinds of 19-year, 235-lunation cycle, mentioned in *Section 8*, two of which are shown in Table V and Table VI, are not separately constructed; they are simply groups of 19 consecutive lines of this Table VII, thus adjusted, with a slight further adjustment at or near the end of each cycle to render it a repeating one.

When line XXV occurs in a 19-year cycle, it borrows the six missing new moons (Feb 5, Apr 5, Jun 3, etc.) with their lunations from line XXIV, unless line XXIV also occurs; in this latter case, line XXV borrows the six missing new moons with their lunations from line XXVI (Feb 4, Apr 4, Jun 2, etc.) thus equivalently restoring its corrective half-day from the first complete lunation to its former position at the end of the year.

All these adjustments may cause a discrepancy of at most one day in the calendar new moon dates as compared with the mean new moon dates; usually there will be perfect agreement.

The remaining 365 different new moon dates of Table VIII are next written in calendar form, every date with its appropriate epact, and on the addition of the dominical letters the New Style yearly calendar is finished. It is shown in Table IX. This is the ecclesiastical yearly calendar; the civil yearly calendar omits the epacts since these appertain solely to the lunar calendar.

The six calendar dates, Feb 5, Apr 5, etc., must each have two epacts, XXV and XXIV, because each of these dates arose from two different years of new moon dates—the years XXV and XXIV (see Table VII). On Feb 4, Apr 4, etc., the epact XXV, written as [25]* is placed with XXVI for a reason to be more fully discussed in *Section 12*.

By this ingenious construction of the yearly calendar a given year contains, depending on its epact, eleven or twelve complete lunations of alternately 30 and 29 days each, or of alternately 29 and 30 days each, plus a number of days at the beginning and at the end of the year.

A given year's epact, while retaining its original meaning as an *excess* and as the *age of the moon* at the beginning of the year (*Section 9*) now assumes a new function: in the yearly calendar it designates the new moon dates during that year.

For example: Let the current epact be XX. This means:

1° The excess at the end of the preceding year, after the last complete lunation was 20 days.

* Or in some other way to distinguish it from XXV or 25.

2° The moon's age at the beginning of the given year is 20 days; the lunation therefore has (30 − 20), or 10 days to go *before* the first new moon of the year.

3° Since the epact XX in the yearly calendar, due to the diminishing order of the epacts, is placed on the eleventh line, it designates Jan 11 as the first new moon date of the year, and, therefore, by the construction of Table VII, Feb 9, Mar 11, etc., as the following new moon dates of the year.

Section 12

The epact [25]. *Three consecutive epacts impossible in the same epact series.*

In the preceding section it was stated that the 19-year cycle proper to a current period is simply an excerpt of some set of 19 consecutive lines of the adjusted 30-year cycle (Table VII), and that line XXV, if it occurs, borrows its six missing lunations from line XXIV, unless this latter line also occurs, in which case line XXV borrows its six missing lunations from line XXVI. This topic will now be continued from the viewpoint of the New Style yearly calendar (Table IX).

The following proposition will be needed:

Of three consecutive epacts, for instance, XXIV, XXV, and XXVI, not more than *two* can occur in the same series of 19 epacts.

Proof. Let an unlimited series of epacts, XI, XXII, III, etc., be formed by the annual addition of 11 days without exception, and the omission of 30 days whenever possible.

Then in any group of 31 of these epacts, there will be 30 additions of 11, and 11 omissions of 30, corresponding to the 11 embolismic lunations (Table VII), and the last epact of the group will be identical with the first epact (E),

because $$E + (30 \times 11) - (11 \times 30) = E$$

Likewise, in any group of nine epacts there will be eight additions of 11, and ($\frac{9}{31} \times 11$), or three omissions of 30, and the last epact of the group will be two smaller than the first,

because $$E + (8 \times 11) - (3 \times 30) = E - 2$$

Finally, in any group of twelve epacts there will be eleven additions of 11, and ($\frac{12}{31} \times 11$), or four omissions of 30, and the last epact of the group will be one larger than the first,

because $$E + (11 \times 11) - (4 \times 30) = E + 1$$

Now let E, E + 1, and E + 2, be the given consecutive epacts. The 9-year group can occur in the 19-year series of epacts in only one way; namely, if E + 2 is followed eight years later by E. The 12-year group can occur either if E is followed eleven years later by E + 1, or if E + 1 is followed eleven years later by E + 2. A combination of two intervals cannot occur; for the smallest combination would contain (11 + 8) or 19 years, and if this is added to the lowest initial golden number (GN = 1), the last of the three given epacts would fall in the twentieth year which is outside the 19-year series. *Q.e.d.*

This proposition leads to the important conclusion: If the epacts XXIV and XXV both occur in the same 19-year series, XXVI cannot occur.

In general, there would be no objection to a calendar date, such as Feb 5, being the new moon date for two lunations belonging to two different years, if both lunations are of equal length; but if they are of unequal length, they will interfere with the letter-number scheme in the Martyrology, to be explained in *Section 14*.

The lunations beginning February 5 in the years XXIV and XXV are of unequal length (Table VIII); likewise the lunations beginning Feb 4 in the years XXVI and [25]. (Tables VIII and VI.)

Now, in the New Style yearly calendar (Table IX), consider the peculiar group of epacts in February:

[25], XXVI, Feb 4
XXV, XXIV, Feb 5

The epact XXVI, if it occurs in the current series of 19 epacts, must be alined with Feb 4, and XXIV with Feb 5, because it is from these two years that the calendar dates arose. A place must therefore be found for XXV if it occurs.

A place is found as follows: XXV is alined with Feb 5, unless XXIV also occurs; in this case, since both epacts cannot have the same new moon date, XXV, written as [25], is alined with Feb 4, replacing XXVI, which in that case cannot occur. The same placement of the missing epact XXV is effected in the other five months, April, June, July, September, November.

So the rule is: The epact XXV is ordinarily used; but when XXIV and XXV both occur in the current series of 19 epacts, [25] is used instead of XXV, both in the New Style yearly calendar (Table IX), and in the two New Style paschal tables (Table X and Table XI) that are to be derived from it, as will be shown in *Section 15*. Such is the case in the present period, 1900 to 2199. (See Table IV.)

The epact [25] can occur only in a year whose golden number is twelve or larger. For it must be *preceded* in its series by XXIV; the interval is eleven years, which added to the lowest possible golden number, results in the twelfth year of the series as the earliest possible one for the epact [25].

Section 13

The epact [19]

We have seen in *Section 8* that the 235-lunation cycle of Meton is used as a measure of time.

The 371-lunation cycle (Table VII) is used solely for the construction of a yearly calendar. It cannot be used as a measure of time, for in its unadjusted form it contains 371 new moons whose duplicate dates cannot be eliminated as in Meton's cycle, by means of the eleven half-days available; and in its adjusted form it lacks six whole lunations and is far shorter than its solar counterpart of 30 common years.

Hence, in any conflict between the two cycles, the former has the right of way, and the latter must be made to agree with it.

Such a conflict arises in a year that simultaneously has the epact XIX and the golden number 19. Table V illustrates this case; it shows that the year whose epact is XIX must end with the new moon on Dec 31, in order to preserve the repeating nature of the 235-lunation cycle. In the adjusted 30-year cycle (Table VII), the year whose epact is XIX has *no* new moon on Dec 31; the year that has the new moon on Dec 31, has the epact XX. Since it was from this cycle, rearranged, that the yearly calendar was constructed, the calendar has XX on the Dec 31 line (Table IX).

In the yearly calendar, therefore, the epact XIX, written as [19], is placed at Dec 31 together with XX, which does not occur in such a cycle (see Table V), and [19] is used only in a year that simultaneously has the epact XIX and the golden number 19. Such years occurred in the period 1582 to 1699 (Table IV) and they will not occur again until about AD 8500. (See Table III.)

Section 14

Epact Letters

In the Roman Martyrology epact letters are used to indicate the daily age of the moon in its current lunation.

We have seen that the epact for a given year indicates in the yearly calendar (Table IX) which days of that year have new moons (*Section 11*).

In the Martyrology every day of the year has a scheme of Arabic numbers from 1 to 29 or 30, designating in general the days of the current lunation.

Now assume that the epact of a given year is III; in the Martyrology on Jan 28, which is the first new moon day of that year (Table IX), the epact III could be printed above the Arabic number 1 to indicate that the current lunation is having its first day or new moon; on Jan 29, III could be printed above 2; on Jan 30, above 3, and so forth, and on any of these days the reader could see at a glance what is the day of the current lunation; for it is

Epact		Letter	Epact	Letter
I	=	a	XVII	s
II		b	XVIII	t
III		c	XIX	u
IV		d	XX	A
V		e	XXI	B
VI		f	XXII	C
VII		g	XXIII	D
VIII		h	XXIV	E
IX		i	[25]	[F]
X		k	XXV	F
XI		l	XXVI	G
XII		m	XXVII	H
XIII		n	XXVIII	M
XIV		p	XXIX	N
XV		q	*	P
XVI		r		

always given by the Arabic number below the epact III. One can easily imagine what the number scheme on a given day would look like, after all the Arabic numbers had all the epacts, including [25], printed above them in their proper places. Some numbers must have double epacts, such as:

[25] XXV; [25] XXVI; XXV, XXVI;

depending on the day of the year.

As a matter of convenience, not the epacts themselves are thus printed, but their equivalents, the epact letters, as given in the table above. So if a year's epact is III, its epact letter is c, below which letter on every day of that year one can read the corresponding day of the current lunation.

The letter-number scheme for Jan 28 is here given as a sample:

a	b	c	d	e	f	g	h	i	k	l	m	n	p	q	r	s	t	u
29	30	1	2	3	4	5	6	7	8	9	10	11	12	13	14	15	16	17

A	B	C	D	E	[F]	F	G	H	M	N	P
18	19	20	21	22	23	23	24	25	26	27	28

The position of the letters remains the same for all days; the Arabic numbers move from right to left one space per day.

It must be remembered, however, that this is the day of the *calendar* lunation; the day of the mean lunation may precede it by as much as two days.

Section 15

Construction of two New Style paschal tables. Three methods for finding New Style Easter dates.

The calendar date on which Easter falls in any given year after 1582, may be found in several ways. It will first be necessary to determine the year's golden number by *Section 2,* its epact by Table IV, and its dominical letter by *Section 3.*

First method, by means of the New Style yearly calendar (Table IX).

The Council of Nicaea defined Easter as the first Sunday after the fourteenth moon that occurs on or after March 21, which is the calendar equinox.

Because the Hebrew month that precedes Nisan, namely Adar, or in embolismic years, Veadar, contains 29 days, the range of the Easter new moon is 29 days, from Mar 8 to Apr 5 (both dates included). The addition of 13 days to each of these limits gives the range of the fourteenth moon of the Easter lunation from Mar 21 to Apr 18. Thirteen days *only* are added because the Easter new moon day is the first day of the Easter lunation.

Hence, to find Easter in any given New Style year by means of the reformed yearly calendar, the epact of that year determines the Easter new moon between Mar 8 and Apr 5 (both included); the addition of 13 days determines the fourteenth moon of the Easter lunation; the current dominical letter next *below* this fourteenth moon gives Easter Sunday.

Example: Find Easter in AD 1938.

We have: GN = 1, Epact = XXIX, DL is B.

In Table IX the epact XXIX between Mar 8 and Apr 5 (both included) is found at Apr 1; this is, therefore, the calendar Easter new moon. The addition of 13 days puts the calendar Easter full moon on Apr 14. The first B *below* Apr 14 points to Easter Sunday on Apr 19.

Second method, by means of the old paschal table, reformed (Table X).

This table is simply an excerpt from the New Style yearly calendar to facilitate the finding of Easter. The epacts of the yearly calendar within the Easter new moon range, Mar 8 to Apr 5, are listed directly with the dominical letters within the range of the fourteenth moon, Mar 21 to Apr 18 and beyond. The second and third column of Table X are usually omitted; they are retained here for the sake of greater clearness.

Hence, to find Easter by means of the old paschal table, reformed, the given year's epact determines in the third column the date of the fourteenth moon within its proper range; the current DL next *below* that date is alined with Easter in the seventh column.

Example: Find Easter in AD 1936.
We have: GN = 18, Epact = VI, DL is ED—a leap year.

In Table X the epact VI shows that Mar 25 is the calendar Easter new moon; Apr 7 is the calendar Easter full moon; the next D *below* Apr 7 points to Easter Sunday on Apr 12.

Third method, by means of the new reformed paschal table (Table XI).

The preceding Table X may be re-arranged with the dominical letter, instead of the epact as the primary argument. For this purpose we note that in Table X

the first D	can follow	XXIII only	with Easter on			Mar 22
the second D	"	"	XXII to XVI	"	"	"	Mar 29
the third D	"	"	XV to IX	"	"	"	Apr 5
the fourth D	"	"	VIII to II	"	"	"	Apr 12
the fifth D	"	"	I to XXVI, [25], XXV, XXIV	"	"	"	Apr 19

After the other letters are treated in the same way, the tabulation of the results leads to the new reformed paschal table (Table XI) and it affords the simplest method of all for finding Easter; but see *Section 28.*

Example: Find Easter in 1936.
We have as above: GN = 18, Epact = VI, DL is ED.

Enter Table XI with D as primary argument; the epact VI in the fourth line of epacts directly determines Apr 12 as Easter.

In Table X and Table XI the *civil* dates of the movable feasts depending on Easter are listed; such lists were compiled for *common* years. In leap years the first dominical letter may be used for Jan–Feb feasts, and the second dominical letter must be used for the Mar–Dec feasts.

A caution is here in place. At very rare intervals a leap year's epact will be XXIV or XXV, standing at the end of the epact column in Table X, and its dominical letters will be DC. When this occurs, the use of the first DL for Jan–Feb feasts will lead to error; the second DL should then be used and the listed dates for Jan–Feb feasts augmented by one day, because of the additional date (Feb 29) in leap years.

Example: In AD 3784 (GN = 4, Epact = XXV, DL is DC), the use of C puts Easter on Apr 25, and therefore Septuagesima correctly on Feb (21 + 1) or Feb 22; whereas the use of D would put this Sunday on Feb 15, which is evidently wrong, since Septuagesima precedes Easter by nine weeks or 63 days.

Section 16

History of the Old Style yearly calendar to 1582

From Meton's time (about BC 432) to AD 1582, the traditional series of epacts corresponding to the series of golden numbers was used; it was never changed. This traditional series is here given:

GN	1	2	3	4	5	6	7	8	9	10	11	12	13
Epact	XI	XXII	III	XIV	XXV	VI	XVII	XXVIII	IX	XX	I	XII	XXIII

GN	14	15	16	17	18	19
Epact	IV	XV	XXVI	VII	XVIII	XXIX

As a preliminary for the introduction of his 19-year cycle, Meton chose a solar common year which he knew from previous observation of new moon dates would begin with a new moon on its first day. As a consequence, this year would end with an excess of (365 − 354) or XI days after the last complete lunation. From these XI "left-over" days, in Greek called ἐπακταὶ ἡμέραι, the XI got its name of epact. Meton wrote this XI before the *following* year, to which he assigned the golden number 1, thus beginning the construction of his 235-lunation cycle, or lunar yardstick. (See *Section 8*.)

He decided that a lunation that extended over the end of one year and the beginning of the next, should always have 30 days. This he did in order that for any year of his cycle, thirty minus the year's epact would indicate the number of days the current lunation still had to run before the first new moon date of that year, and thirty-one minus the year's epact would give that first new moon date.

So, the first year of Meton's cycle had GN = 1. Epact = XI, and the first new moon occurred on the (31 − XI), or on the twentieth day of that year. To avoid decimal parts of a day, the following lunations were given alternately 29 and 30 days each, thus averaging $29\frac{1}{2}$ days, a practical approximate value of a mean lunation. The first year ended, of course, with (XI + XI) or XXII "left-over" days, so that the next year had GN = 2, Epact = XXII, with the first new moon on the (31 − XXII), or the ninth day.

This second year contained one lunation more than the first, and ended with III "left-over" days. But the lunation current at the year's end would have had only 29 days. Here is where the first corrective half-day had to be applied in order to give that lunation ($29\frac{1}{2} + \frac{1}{2}$) or 30 days. Proceeding thus to the end of his cycle and adding the corrective half-day at the *end* of of the year, whenever it was needed, Meton found that he required *seven* half-days in his lunar cycle; namely, at the end of the years, GN = 2, 5, 8, 10, 13, 16, and 19.

On the completion of his cycle, Meton took an ordinary common year calendar then in use, and at every one of its calendar dates, if it occurred in his cycle, he wrote the corresponding golden number (or epact). He worked either with golden numbers or with epacts; in all Old Style tables in this book both are given for the sake of completeness.

He noticed that there were six pairs of identical new moon dates in his cycle—in the years, GN = 11 and 19, and that the spacing of the golden numbers (or epacts) in his yearly calendar was rather irregular. He ingeniously eliminated the identity of new moon dates by shifting the corrective half-day from the end of the year GN = 19 to the first complete lunation in that year, making it a ($29\frac{1}{2} + \frac{1}{2}$) or 30-day lunation, to be followed by 29, 30, etc., to the end of the year; the current lunation at the year's end still contained 30 days. By treating the years, GN = 5, 8, and 16 in the same way he regularized to a great extent the spacing in his yearly calendar.

In the construction of his cycle Meton had to use *seven* half-days; he knew from theory that only five half-days were available. (See *Section 8*.) He made up for the two over-corrections that he had applied in the years whose GN = 16 and 19, by subtracting one day from the lunation current at the end of the last year (GN = 19) of his cycle, giving that lunation (30 − 1) or 29 days. This made his lunar cycle a *repeating* one.

To make his epact series a repeating series, Meton saw that 12 days (instead of 11) would have to be added to the last epact XXIX.

Meton's work was done; he had produced a perpetual yearly calendar on which, with the use of a given year's golden number (or epact), one could read the new moon dates of that year, with the lunations alternating, as they should, between 29 and 30 days. Not many centuries, however, elapsed before it became apparent that his perpetual yearly calendar was not as perpetual as he had thought; the observed new moons no longer occurred on their indicated calendar dates!

In BC 44, at Julius Caesar's behest, Sosigenes reformed the Roman Calendar both in its solar and in its lunar part. In the former he decided among other things that *every* fourth year thereafter should be a leap year. In the latter, he corrected Meton's yearly calendar to make its new moon dates agree with recently observed new moons, but he retained the traditional epact series.

Then, instead of the Greek subdivisions of the calendar year, that Meton had used, he substituted Roman months, whose names are familiar to us, together with their Kalends, Nones, and Ides, and the clumsy way of numbering their days. Much later, in the twelfth century, the simpler Arabic notation, used throughout this study, was brought to Europe.

Sosigenes found that Meton's first year, GN = 1, Epact = XI, had its first new moon on Mar 23 of the Romanized form of the yearly calendar. Beginning with these data, he constructed, as Meton had done, a 235-lunation cycle, shown in Table XII. The epacts had now lost their original meaning of "left-over" days, and thirty-four minus a year's epact (diminished by 30 when possible) indicated the first new moon date of that year. (See Table XII.)

Sosigenes next entered the golden numbers (or epacts) of his cycle at their proper calendar dates in a common year Roman calendar, the year beginning on Mar 1, as shown in Table XIII. This, his yearly calendar, remained in use to 1582.

The Old Style year, therefore, began on Mar 1; it was then that the golden number (or epact) of the preceding year was changed. This fact explains several anomalies in our present common year calendar, which begins with Jan 1.

1° July, August, and February each originally had 30 days, and February was the last month of the year. One day was added to July, the month named after Julius Caesar, to make it equal in length to any other month; the month of August, named after his successor Augustus Caesar, also received an additional day for a like reason. Both these days were taken from the end of the year, leaving February with only twenty eight days.

2° Before leap years the intercalary day was naturally added in February, then the last month of the year.

3° The seventh month of the Old Style year was rightly named September, . . . etc., the tenth month, December. When, in 1582, the year was made to begin on January 1, these four names of months were retained, though now inappropriate, since September was now the ninth month, . . . etc.

To return to antiquity. When the Christians in the Roman Empire began to use the Old Style yearly calendar (see Table XIII) to determine their Easter date, no change was necessary because the irregularity of the spacing of the golden numbers (or epacts) in April fell outside the range of the Easter new moons, Mar 8 to Apr 5 (both included). From the Old Style yearly calendar, the Old Style paschal table, shown in Table XIV, was formed, exactly as Table X was later on formed from Table IX, as explained in *Section 15*. The epacts contained in Table XIV are, of course, *traditional epacts*. It is seen that from the earliest times to 1582, Easter dates could be determined by means either of golden numbers or of traditional epacts. As a matter of fact, in the Old Style yearly calendar and in the paschal table derived from it, the traditional epacts were usually omitted and only golden numbers were used. With the passing of the centuries, the golden numbers in the yearly calendar no longer indicated the correct new moon dates as of old; the yearly calendar gradually got into a frightful mess,* but it was not changed until 1582.

SECTION 17

Old Style Easter Dates

THERE ARE three methods for finding an Easter date before 1582. An example will illustrate them.

Example: Find Easter of AD 526.
We have: GN = 14 (*Sect. 2*); DL is D (*Section 3*).

First method, by means of the Old Style yearly calendar (Table XIII). The GN 14 within the range Mar 8 to Apr 5 (both included) puts the Easter new moon for that year on Mar 30; the addition of 13 days puts the fourteenth moon on Apr 12, and the first D *below* Apr 12 gives Apr 19 as Easter Sunday.

Second method, by means of the Old Style paschal table (Table XIV). The GN 14 determines the line; the first D *below* that line points to Apr 19 as Easter.

* In the sixteenth century the calendar new moons regularly lagged from three to five days behind their respective mean new moons, with the result that, from 1500 to 1582, in twelve years Easter was celebrated one lunation later than Leviticus 23:5 would require, and in many other years Easter was celebrated one week too late.

However, it is not necessary to determine a pre-reformation Easter in this ancient way by means of the Old Style yearly calendar or paschal table. Though 30 epacts were not then in use, one may nevertheless use them to find a pre-reformation Easter in combination with the New Style yearly calendar (Table IX), or with one of the New Style paschal tables (Table X or Table XI). For this purpose we may use a series of *reformed* epacts, taken from the theoretical part of Table III; it is the series

VIII, XIX, ✳, XI, . . . etc.

that would have applied to the first century of the Christian Era, had the Gregorian Reform then been in force. This series is listed for this express purpose in Table IV for years preceding 1582.

Third method, by means of reformed epacts.
In the given example we have: GN = 14, Epact = I (Table IV); DL is D.

By any of the three methods given in *Section 15,* it is seen that Easter fell on Apr 19.

The same caution is necessary in the use of Table XIV as was given at the end of *Section 15.*

Example. Find Septuagesima Sunday in AD 1204.
We have: GN = 8, DL is DC, a *leap* year.
The GN 8 in Table XIV determines the line; the first C *below* that line puts Septuagesima correctly on Feb (21 + 1) or Feb. 22. If D were used, it would put this Sunday erroneously on Feb 15.

The Greek Orthodox Church never adopted the Gregorian Reform; it still follows the unreformed Julian Calendar. Orthodox Easters are, therefore, determined as they were prior to 1582, by means of the given year's golden number and its Old Style dominical letter, used with Table XIV. But the resulting Orthodox Easter date is a Julian, or Old Style date; in the present period (1900 to 2199), this Julian date may be converted into the equivalent Gregorian date by the addition of 13 days, corresponding to the total number of days hitherto dropped in the Gregorian, but not in the Julian Calendar.

Example: The year 1941 has the golden number 4, and the Old Style dominical letter F, derived by Formula I of *Section 3*; by Table XIV the Orthodox Easter of this year is on Apr 7 (Julian), or on Apr (7 + 13) or Apr 20 (Gregorian). Using the golden number 4, the epact II, and the New Style dominical letter E, one finds by Table X that the Gregorian Easter is on April 13, thus preceding the Orthodox Easter by one week.

A similar comparison of results for a number of years shows that the Orthodox Easter may coincide with the Gregorian Easter, or it may lag behind it by one, four, or five weeks, depending on the interplay of golden numbers and dominical letters of the successive years; no general rule can be given.

Easter dates in the East before the Council of Nicaea (325), and in the Roman Church before 525, and in the British Isles before 664, are uncertain, not mathematically—for our tables all go back to the beginning of the Era—but historically because of the Easter controversies. (*Section 7.*)

The diversity of early cycles used in the West influenced the determination of Easter in some years. The accusation against Pope St. Symmachus* affords an instance. In AD 501 (GN = 8), following the older cycle then used at Rome, he celebrated Easter on Mar 25, whereas his opponents at Rome, the Laurentians, following the Greek cycle, celebrated Easter that year on Apr 22, and accused him before the Emperor at Constantinople of anticipating the Easter festival.

Such discrepancy of four weeks in the celebration of Easter regularly occurred every 19 years—in years that had the golden number 8; but shorter discrepancies of a week were frequent in other years, due to the various combinations of golden numbers and dominical letters. This incident probably occasioned the abandonment of the old cycle at Rome, and the adoption of Meton's 19-year cycle in AD 525.

Meanwhile (AD 457) Victorius† of Aquitaine had introduced a new paschal cycle into Gaul. Since his cycle was an exact multiple of nineteen, containing as it did (19 × 28) or 532 years, its results were not necessarily defective; the main objection to it was its excessive length. Its use continued in Gaul to Charlemagne's time (AD 800). Thereafter, both East and West used the simple 19-year cycle of Meton to determine Easter, as is done to this day.

The older paschal cycles cannot be mathematically reconstructed with any degree of probability, for lack of sufficient historical data.

Section 18

The Reform of the Old Style Yearly Calendar in 1582

THE CALENDAR-REFORMERS in 1582 decided to have the year begin on Jan 1 instead of Mar 1, as previously; this they did in order to bring Septua-

* See *Catholic Encyclopedia, s. v.*
† *Op. cit.*, Vol. VI, p. 360.

gesima Sunday and Ash Wednesday into the *same* calendar year as the Easter day for which these days were a preparation. For this purpose they worked back from Mar 1, carefully observing the proper spacing of the golden numbers (or epacts) in Table XIII, and found that Jan 1 would have GN = 3, Epact = III, the same as Mar 1.

They next removed the golden numbers entirely from their yearly calendar because they found them unsuited for a perpetual letter-number scheme in the Martyrology. These golden numbers they put in a separate table, like Table IV.

Then, noticing that the traditional epacts in their yearly calendar decreased with remarkable regularity, they decided to fill out the spaces between the traditional epacts with eleven new epacts, making (19 + 11) or 30 epacts in all; they thus had one for every day of the calendar year. They were confronted with three obstacles that had to be overcome:

1° There was no epact available for the space between I and XXIX; the epact XXX would not do, because thirty days is a complete lunation and could not be "left-over" days, according to the original definition of an epact. So they used the asterisk ✳ instead of XXX, understanding it was to mean either zero or thirty, whichever meaning was momentarily more convenient in their work. It must be remembered that the Roman notation had no symbol for zero.

2° In six of the months there was no space for the epact XXVII (see April in Table XIII). This difficulty led to the study of the 30-year cycle of new moon dates (Table VII) with its clever scheme for the placement of a missing epact (see *Section 11* and *Section 12*).

3° The disturbing combination of three epacts thus formed, fell partly at the end, and partly at the beginning of the calendar range of the Easter new moon (Mar 8 to Apr 5, both included). See Table XIII. To overcome this difficulty they subtracted three from every epact in their yearly calendar, and by shifting the corrective half-day from the end to near the beginning of each of the six years, ✳ to XXV (see Table VIII), they caused XXV to be the missing epact in six of the months. This conveniently brought the disturbing combination of three epacts, which could not be entirely avoided, at the *end* of the Easter new moon range*), and the reduction of every epact by three days had the further advantage of restoring all thirty epacts to the original meaning of "left-over" days. (See *Section 19*.)

Their yearly calendar was now finished and had the form of the New Style yearly calendar given in Table IX.

* Any one of the epacts XXIX to XX can be made the missing epact in the six critical months of the year by shifting more or fewer of the corrective half-days from the end to near the beginning of the corresponding years. (See Table VIII.)

The reformers then brought the daily letter-number scheme in the old Martyrology into agreement with the reformed yearly calendar. Previously, 19 small letters of the alphabet had represented golden numbers (or traditional epacts); 11 capital letters were added and all 30 letters were thereafter to represent reformed epacts *only*, as shown in *Section 14*, and the distinction between [F] and F was introduced. The new edition of the Martyrology, embodying these changes in the daily letter-number scheme, was issued by Pope Gregory XIII in 1584.

Finally, to restore the mean vernal equinox to the calendar date Mar 21, the position it had held in AD 325 when the Council of Nicaea defined Easter, the reformers at first thought to drop only nine days (see Table III) from the solar calendar, and to have Oct 14 immediately follow Oct 5, in 1582. However, the corrections needed by the imperfect solar calendar (see Table II) would then put the mean equinox in some years on the calendar date Mar 22. To avoid this and to have spring begin never later than Mar 21 by the calendar, they decided to drop Oct 14 too, thereby adding one day to the solar calendar, and they used this day to diminish by one day every correction due to the calendar during the 400-year cycle. (Table II.) The mean equinox can therefore occur at the latest on (Mar 21.00 plus 0.48) or on Mar 21.48, and at the earliest on (Mar 21.00 minus 1.72) or on Mar 19.28. To perpetuate these conditions for all time to come, the Gregorian Rule was devised.

It would be incorrect to say that the dropping of ten days, instead of nine, corrected the solar calendar to what it had been in the third century of our Era, when the mean vernal equinox coincided with Mar 22, because the extra day added to the calendar by dropping Oct 14 in 1582, was not used to bring the mean vernal equinox to Mar 22, where it had been when Easter was not yet defined, but it was used, as stated, to diminish by one day all the annual corrections needed by the imperfect solar calendar. The date Mar 21 was therefore retained as the calendar equinox, as it had been in the year 325, and had remained throughout all the following centuries, while Mar 12 was approaching the mean equinox, which position it reached in the sixteenth century before the reform.

Those ten days that were dropped from the solar calendar because of the mean vernal equinox, had to be applied to the lunar calendar as a solar equation of like amount, because the new moon dates are given in solar time; this reduced the series of traditional epacts

XI, XXII, III, . . . etc.

to the series of reformed epacts

I, XII, XXIII, . . . etc.,

which was to be in use from the reform to 1699. (See Table IV.)

The series of traditional epacts, having been on duty since Meton's time, was now relegated to the reserves; its time of service will come again in AD 6200 (or in 5900 if the year 4800 is to be a common year). (See Table III and *Section 24*.)

So, in the Gregorian Calendar we have as a result of the reform:

1° The mean vernal equinox either falls on Mar 21, or precedes that date by not more than two days.

2° A mean new moon either falls on the same day as the corresponding calendar new moon, or it precedes the latter by not more than two days. When there is a discrepancy, it amounts to but a few hours either way; it occurs very rarely, and it is consequently here disregarded. (See *Section 19*.)

A calendar cannot, of course, take into account the effect of perturbations on the phases of the apparent (true) moon, or on the time of the true vernal equinox, though in the case of the latter, the Gregorian calendar allows sufficient leeway—over half a day.

SECTION 19

The History of the Calendar (continued)

THE OMISSION of a lunar equation when due, *increases* by one day the maximum lag of a calendar new moon behind its mean new moon. To realize this important fact, consider the period beginning with 2400 in Table III. If the lunar equation then due were omitted, the epact for a year whose GN = 1 would be XXVII, instead of XXVIII. Since the epacts are written in *inverted* order in the yearly calendar (Table IX), the first calendar new moon in that year would be on Jan 4, instead of Jan 3, that is, the lag would be increased by one day. Since the total range of the lag is three days, the whole range of the lag would be shifted one day.

It is easy enough to reconstruct Meton's work on the lunar calendar, described in *Section 16*. He left it under the spell of his equation:

$$31 - \text{epact} = \text{the first new moon of the Greek year}$$

in which equation the epact is true to its original definition of "left-over days" of the preceding year.

It is impossible to follow Sosigenes in all the details of his work. The following is certain:

1° The traditional series of epacts was never changed from Meton's time to 1582.

2° There had been a lunar equation neglected in the year BC 100, thus increasing the maximum lag of Meton's calendar new moons by one day.

3° Sosigenes converted the Greek year into the Roman year beginning Mar 1.

4° He *increased* every new moon date, expressed in terms of the resulting Roman year by three days; for he changed Meton's equation to the form:

$$34 - \text{epact} = \text{first new moon of the Roman year.}$$

For, when in an equation of the form: $M - S = R$, the subtrahend (S) remains unchanged, and the minuend (M) is increased by three, the remainder (R) is necessarily increased by three. This means that he effectively lowered the golden number-epact column in his yearly calendar three lines. The traditional epacts now no longer satisfied their original definition.

5° Mar 23 was the first calendar new moon date of the year whose GN = 1, Epact = XI in the Romanized form of the yearly calendar; for thus it remained until 1582.

6° His maximum lag of the calendar new moon behind the mean new moon was zero; this follows from the reformers' work in 1582, to be described below.

The following is uncertain:

1° What was the maximum lag of Meton's calendar new moon dates?

2° When did Meton's Greek year begin?

Until these two points are cleared up, it is impossible to itemize all that Sosigenes did to Meton's lunar calendar.

After Sosigenes' time, lunar equations were neglected in AD 200, 500, 800, 1100, and 1400, each of which increased the maximum lag by one day. Three of these had been allowed for in the letter-number scheme of the Martyrology, but not in the lunar calendar. Sosigenes' equation:

$$34 - \text{epact} = \text{first new moon date of the year,}$$

was applied until 1582, but after AD 200 it gave results ever more incorrect with the passing centuries; by 1500, Sosigenes' maximum lag of zero had been increased by five days!

The reformers let two of those five neglected lunar equations go uncorrected, in order to retain a maximum lag of two days. Hence, the calendar new moon can *now* never *precede* its mean new moon, but either coincides with it, or follows it to the extent of two days. The remaining three neglected lunar equations, the reformers applied by raising the epact column in the yearly calendar three lines; this diminished every calendar new moon date by three days, and Sosigenes' equation:

$$34 - \text{epact} = \text{first new moon date of the year}$$

was now restored to its original Metonic form:

$$31 - \text{epact} = \text{first new moon date of the year}$$

and has remained so ever since; the epacts were thereby restored to their original meaning as "left-over days."

The shifting of the year's beginning from Mar 1 to Jan 1 caused no change in the epacts; this was unique and, so to say, accidental. Any other shift of the beginning of the year, for instance to May 1, would have entailed a change of epacts, or a change in Meton's equation, with the consequent loss of their original definition.

The lunar calendar was now finished with the following results:

1° The traditional epact series was still in use.
2° The epacts were restored to their original definition.
3° Meton's equation was restored.
4° The solar year, in the terms of which new moon dates are expressed, began on Jan 1.

There was another problem awaiting solution, and it had nothing to do directly with the lunar calendar; the date Mar 21 of the solar calendar had to be restored to the mean vernal equinox, where it had stood in the fourth century, when the Council of Nicaea defined Easter. In order that the maximum two days' lag of the calendar Easter New moons within their range, Mar 8 to Apr 5 (both included) might not be increased, but rather counteracted, at least in part, by the lag of Mar 21 behind the mean vernal equinox, so that the Easter lunation determined by the calendar would always be "the first month of the year," in accordance with Leviticus (23:5), it was decided to drop ten days (instead of nine) from the solar calendar, as explained in *Section 18*.

In order not to disturb the corrected lunar calendar, whose new moon dates are expressed in solar time, these ten days had to be applied to it as a solar equation, as stated in the preceding section; they were subtracted from the traditional epact series—the first time in recorded history that such a thing was done!

Three days, therefore, had been added to the lunar calendar and ten days had been subtracted, resulting in an effective subtraction of *seven* days, thus effectively restoring the lunar calendar to the condition it would have been in at the beginning of our Era, had the Gregorian reform then been in force; for, the reformed epact series for AD 0 would have been (by Table III):

VIII, XIX, ✳, XI, . . . etc.

and the subtraction of seven days from each would give:

I, XII, XXIII, IV, . . . etc.

which is the reformed series for the period 1582 to 1699, obtained by subtracting ten days from the traditional series:

XI, XXII, III, XIV, . . . etc.

The history of any luni-solar calendar would be incomplete without a brief account of the saros. This is an important period of 6585.321124 days, roughly equal to 18 calendar years and $11\frac{1}{3}$ days, during which 223 apparent new moons occur at the same intervals apart, as in the previous similar period. It is caused by a complete rotation within that period of the major axis of the moon's elliptic orbit relatively to the major axis of the earth's elliptic orbit.

The saros serves to compute eclipses either of the sun or of the moon, and is used as follows: To the initial eclipse year add 18; to the initial day of the month add 11 (10, if the initial eclipse occurred in Mar–Dec before a leap year, or in Jan–Feb in a leap year); to the initial eclipse time of day add 0.321124 days, or 7 hours, 42 minutes, 25 seconds. The result is the date of the corresponding following eclipse. It was thus that the Babylonians predicted eclipses long before Meton's time.

The saros may be used in the same way to determine *any* apparent new moon, whether attended by an eclipse or not, from the corresponding new moon 18 years before, and was probably so used by the ancients.

For example: There was an apparent new moon

1926, Jan 14, 6 hours, 34 minutes, 42 seconds G.C.M.T.;

there will therefore be a new moon

1944, Jan 25, 14 hours, 17 minutes, 7 seconds.

The perturbations of the moon's, and of the earth's motion, due to the attraction of the other planets, will slightly modify such results.

A single saros would have given in antiquity a rather accurate value of the *mean* lunation. Assume that the ancients had measured the time interval between two corresponding eclipses of the moon, observing in the case of each the time of the first and of the last contact, and taking the average of both contacts as the center of the eclipse, or the exact moment of full moon. Assume that they thus found the value of the saros to be 6585 days, thereby committing an error of 0.321124 days, or almost 8 hours. They had no pendulum clocks for the accurate measurement of time, and the contacts are hard to distinguish; still they could probably have done better than we have assumed, considering the four, or even eight contacts observed. Division of 0.321124 by 223 gives 0.00144 as the error of a mean lunation derived from their observations—about 2 minutes. They would have regarded 6585 ÷ 223, or 29.529148 days as a mean lunation, instead of 29.530588 days, which is the correct value.

Having thus determined the mean lunation, they would naturally have applied it to calendar work, for which the saros itself is unsuited because of the inequality of its apparent lunations. A basic mean new moon date they could have found by taking the median value of the 223 apparent new moon dates of a saros.

If these seem to be bold assumptions, one must remember that the mathematical ingenuity of the ancients is often underrated; their luni-solar calendars show that they had a comprehensive knowledge of the intricate factors involved, as the reader of these pages has no doubt by this time concluded for himself.

It was by the study of the saros that Meton probably came to discover his own cycle. Noticing that the 11 days by which the saros exceeded 18 calendar years equalled 365 − 354), or one common year less twelve $29\frac{1}{2}$-day lunations, he was led to add one common year to the 18 years, and twelve $29\frac{1}{2}$-day lunations to the 223 apparent lunations of the saros, and suspected that 19 calendar years would equal 235 mean lunations; a little figuring convinced him that it indeed seemed to be so. (See *Section 8* and *Section 10.*)

Section 20

The Story of the Calendar

It was a red-letter day at Athens when Meton announced the discovery that was to immortalize his name. We enter his studio and find him explaining his discovery to a group of learned men. They all agree that it is wonderful and that it will shed great glory on their beloved city; they all agree that a system of measuring time should be based on it; they also agree on the initial year for its introduction. But that is where harmony ends and strife begins.

It was usual in ancient Greece for parties to form, holding opposite views on all questions under the sun; so here, in Meton's studio, some proposed to do their computing by means of the nineteen golden numbers.

"No," said others, "epacts are more mysterious, and therefore more learned. We know when the first new moon occurs next year, so we know what epact to begin with. Let's use epacts!" As they could not agree, each began to figure in his own way.

And first of all, the golden-number-people, and the epact-people, composed a lunar cycle of 235 lunations, and adjusted it for the $2\frac{1}{2}$ days required by the discovery. Then they copied their tables in a neat calendar form, assigning the proper golden numbers, or in the case of the epact-people, the proper epacts to the new moon dates occurring in their lunar cycle.

It must be acknowledged that the golden-number-people had the greater success with their work, for their calendars had many advantages and were used by almost every one during many centuries; whereas the epact calendars never became popular, and the epacts themselves were remembered by only a few highbrows in the intellectual world. But the wrangling between the parties continued down the ages.

Then came the calendar reformers of 1582. "Something must be done about both your calendars," they cried. "It cannot go on like this forever! Spring begins many days too soon, and matters are getting worse from year to year. We need a lunar yardstick that is flexible, one that can adapt itself to the solar and lunar equations as these become necessary—not a cast iron yardstick like the one that both of you use."

This was a stunning blow for the golden-number-people, from which they have never recovered; for they had to confess that their pet golden numbers could not adapt themselves to all of the new requirements.

The epact-people were equally bewildered, because so many days of their calendar were without epacts. But the reformers espoused their cause, and hastened to fill in the empty places in their calendar with other epacts, like a general sending fresh troops to the front.

They even invented a brand new epact. "We need thirty," they said, "and we have only twenty-nine; XXX cannot be used as an epact, because thirty days is a full lunation, and people will wonder why it wasn't dropped at the end of the preceding year. So we'll use the asterisk instead; it means practically the same thing, but doesn't look quite so bad."

Next they tabulated the 19 epacts that were hoary with age, having been born in Meton's time, or even earlier, and they numbered them from one to 19 in the order in which they occur; and when ten days had to be dropped from the solar calendar, in order not to destroy the equality of the two yardsticks, the solar and the lunar, they subtracted ten days from each of these 19 tabulated epacts to obtain substitutes for future use. This they were able to do because they now had 30 epacts at their command.

Still they were not satisfied. From the old yearly epact calendar they boldly sheared the column of epacts, and pasted it back in place with every epact three lines higher than before; this they did to give their new epact, the asterisk, the place of honor at the head of the yearly calendar, alining it with Jan 1, for they had resolved that this date should everywhere be regarded as the beginning of the calendar year. Incidentally, by this shift of the whole epact column, they made the epacts conform to their name, as all good epacts should. If one enquires where the three days came from that were added to the lunar calendar by this shift of the epacts, the answer is easy.

They were the three lunar equations that should have been added to the lunar calendar in AD 800, 1100, and 1400, but had been neglected as far as the calendar was concerned.

By all these changes the lunar calendar was, in effect, corrected to what it should have been at the beginning of the Christian Era, whereas the solar calendar was corrected only to the time of the Council of Nicaea.

And when the task was done, the epact-people themselves hardly recognized their traditional yearly calendar.

As to the golden numbers, it must be admitted that they were treated rather shabbily; for they were unceremoniously ousted from the yearly calendar, and relegated to a special department, where they are to find casual employment only once a year in selecting the leading epact, while the steady jobs, so to speak, in calendar work, are monopolized by the epacts throughout the entire year.

Section 21

The Intercalary Day in Leap Years. Civil versus Ecclesiastical Calendar.

Both yearly calendars, the old and the new, and all the cyclical lunar tables, in order to be permanent, are necessarily based on *common* years, because leap years with their intercalary days—an essential part of both yardsticks—do not occupy the same positions in the recurring cycles, either solar or lunar.

It will now be shown how the intercalary day is added to a leap year *without disturbing* the solar calendars and the lunar tables.

Immediately after Feb 23 of a leap year, 24 hours are inserted in the solar calendar, but they are not treated as a separate day; they form together with the following 24 hours, *one single* 48-hour day,* namely Feb 24,

* This 48-hour day of the month comprises, of course, *two* week days that are not so combined.

having in the reformed calendar the dominical letter F, and the epact V. After the first (intercalated) half of this double day, the dominical letter, current for the first part of the leap year, is replaced by the preceding letter of the alphabet for the rest of the year, D becoming C, etc. This is done to maintain the sequence of the weeks. The intercalated half of Feb 24 compensates for the previous four years and prevents the accumulation of those yearly deficiencies, now amounting to almost one whole day, from interfering with the proper date for the coming Easter new moon and Easter Sunday.

At the same time in the cyclical lunar tables, the lunation that contains this 48-hour Feb 24 also receives an additional 24 hours. This explains what was said in *Section 8:* that *apparently* every 235-lunation cycle contains only 6935 days, having been constructed on the basis of 19 common years, but that in reality each cycle contains 6939.75 days; for some of those 6935 days (4 or 5 in every cycle)* are 48-hour days.

In this way one day in every leap year is *simultaneously* added to the solar calendar and to the cyclical lunar tables without disturbing them. The alternative would be to change the yearly solar calendar every fourth year, as is done in the civil calendar by the addition of Feb 29, and to reconstruct all the cyclical lunar tables every nineteen years, which would be prohibitive. The use of a (4 × 19) or 76-year cycle would be undesirable because of its excessively long lunar tables.

The civil calendar is exclusively solar, hence it omits the golden numbers and the epacts; it inserts the intercalary day as February 29, after which the dominical letter is changed.

To avoid errors towards the end of February in leap years, *ecclesiastical* dates must be used with an ecclesiastical calendar. (Table IX.) For this purpose the *civil* dates Feb 25 to Feb 29 should first be changed into the corresponding ecclesiastical dates by the subtraction of one day from each before entering the ecclesiastical calendar.

In like manner, the ecclesiastical dates Feb 24 (latter half) to Feb 28, found from the ecclesiastical calendar may be changed to the corresponding civil dates by *adding* one day to each. At other times of the leap year and in common years the civil and ecclesiastical dates are identical and cause no difficulty.

Example: Let a given leap year have AG as dominical letters. Then Feb

* A single Metonic cycle will contain, sometimes four, sometimes five intercalary days. The lunar yardstick in *Section 8* must therefore be understood to have an *average* length of 6939.75 days. In four such Metonic cycles there will be (4 × 4.75) or 19 intercalary days, corresponding to (4 × 19) or 76 years.

28 (civil) = Feb 27 (ecclesiastical), and it will be a Tuesday; as is shown by the position of G in the ecclesiastical calendar.

Again, G in the ecclesiastical calendar points to Feb 25 (ecclesiastical) as the last Sunday in the month; this will be Feb 26 (civil).

The same results could be obtained directly by the use of the letter A with civil dates, and a civil calendar having the proper dominical letters, but such a civil calendar is not always available.

Ecclesiastical Calendar			Civil Calendar	
Epact	DL	Feb	Feb	DL
XII	F	17	17	F
XI	G	18	18	G
X	A	19	19	A
IX	B	20	20	B
VIII	C	21	21	C
VII	D	22	22	D
VI	E	23	23	E
V	F	24	24	F
			25	G
IV	G	25	26	A
III	A	26	27	B
II	B	27	28	C
I	C	28	29	D
		Mar	Mar	
*	D	1	1	D
XXIX	E	2	2	E
XXVIII	F	3	3	F
XXVII	G	4	4	G
XXVI	A	5	5	A

It might occur to one that a century year not divisible by 400 might be reduced to a common year by a reverse fiction, that would treat a 48-hour Feb 24 as a 24-hour day. Such is not the case; for the yearly calendars and the lunar tables were constructed, not on the assumption of every fourth year being a leap year, but on the assumption that *all* years are common years.

Hence, with the exception of the intercalary days of leap years, the only way to add a day to the lunar calendar, or to subtract a day from it without disturbing the yearly calendar and the lunar tables, is to apply the lunar or the solar equation, and obtain a *new* series of epacts and therewith a new lunar cycle, equal in length to the old one, but of different structure. (*Section 8.*)

Section 22

Mean Easter new moon defined. The lag of the Calendar Easter new moon. The Passover in AD *33.*

Both the Jewish Passover and the Christian Easter received a *calendar* definition, not an astronomical one; and the time of their occurrence is expressed in whole days only, not in decimal parts of a day.

The words of Leviticus enjoining Passover are: "The first month (of the year), the fourteenth day of the month between evenings is the passover of the Lord." (Lev. 23:5, and parallel passages, in the Hebrew text). The Council of Nicaea defined Easter as the Sunday after the fourteenth moon that occurs on or after March 21. The first moon of this Easter lunation is the calendar Easter new moon.

Since a calendar new moon does not necessarily fall on the same day as its corresponding mean new moon, the question arises: "Can not the mean Easter new moon be defined astronomically with reference to the mean vernal equinox?" The question must be answered in the negative, principally because the mean tropical year does not contain an exact number of days. Every year there is a fraction of a day (0.2422) left over, and these fractions accumulate and can be only approximately allowed for at stated intervals by the addition of an intercalary day to the yearly calendar. (See Table II.) The result is that the mean vernal equinox does not fall on the same calendar day year after year, and therefore a purely astronomical definition of the mean Easter new moon is out of the question.

Even the range of the calendar Easter new moon, Mar 8 to Apr 5 (both included), is not decisive. In some years there is no mean new moon within this range; thus in 1932 (see Table XVI) the mean Easter new moon is on Mar 7.85, not on Apr 6.38 one lunation later, both new moons being outside the range; while in 3955 the mean Easter new moon is the one on Apr 6.23, not the preceding new moon on Mar 7.70.

Again, at rare intervals a mean new moon may fall within the range, without however being the mean Easter new moon; thus in 2372 the mean Easter new moon is on Mar 6.31—two days outside the range—and the following mean new moon on Apr 4.84, though well within the range, is not the Easter new moon.

In all such cases, which of the two mean new moons near the limits of the range must be regarded as the Easter new moon depends entirely on the Gregorian Lunar Calendar, and not on the proximity of either moon, to the extremes of the range; neither is the Easter new moon determined by its proximity to the vernal equinox.

In general, there is no necessity for a yearly calendar to be tied to the mean vernal equinox. The Mohammedan Calendar, followed in all Moslem countries, pays no attention to it; a particular month such as Ramadan, may at one time fall in midsummer, and sixteen years later it will have retrograded to midwinter. The Julian Calendar, because of its quadriennial leap years, was originally thought to be anchored to the mean vernal equinox; however, while in the first century of our Era, Mar 24 stood at the equinox, by AD 325 Mar 21, and by 1500 Mar 12 had come to occupy that position. Thus, the yearly calendar moved counterclockwise with respect to the equinox at the rate of three days every 400 years. (See *Section 5.*) Therefore, if the connection of the Gregorian yearly calendar with the mean vernal equinox is not exactly what some critics might wish it to be, so much the worse for the vernal equinox!

Nevertheless, the reformers in 1582 had regard to the mean vernal equinox, as explained in *Section 18*, and tied the Gregorian yearly calendar *loosely* to it, with the result that the yearly calendar, like a huge graduated ring along the ecliptic, keeps pace with the westward movement of the mean vernal equinox and shares in its annual precession of 50.24 seconds of arc. Hence, it can never happen that July, for instance, will ever be a winter month in the northern hemisphere. But the connection is unavoidably a loose one, allowing the yearly calendar to swing to and fro within narrow limits about the mean vernal equinox, like a ship about its mooring. The consequent range of the equinox over three calendar days is disconcerting, but there is no practical remedy.

A purely astronomical definition of the mean Easter new moon is essentially impossible, because no yearly calendar that counts whole days only, and adds corrective days at stated intervals—and no other calendar is conceivable—can be *rigidly* attached to the mean vernal equinox, and without such rigid attachment an astronomical bridge between the mean Easter new moon and the mean equinox cannot be built. Failure to grasp this fact has been the most frequent cause of criticism of the Gregorian Calendar, and has led to the statement that in some years the Calendar puts the Easter festival in the wrong lunation. Such is not the case, for the simple reason that the mean Easter new moon is astronomically undefined.

The only definition possible is the following: The mean Easter new moon is the one that either falls on the same day as the calendar Easter new moon, or precedes it by at most two days (plus a few hours at very rare intervals). This is the only possible definition and it is not an astronomical, but a calendar one.

It would be extremely easy to reduce to zero the maximum lag of calendar new moons behind their corresponding mean new moons; the application of a lunar equation of plus two days, giving rise to a new series of epacts (Table III) would turn the trick. But it would serve no useful purpose because the mean new moons would then have a maximum lag of two days behind their calendar new moons; and, most important of all, because Easter and Passover would thereafter fall on the same day almost every time that Passover falls on a Sunday. This is precisely what the Council of Nicaea, because of the heretical view of some contemporaries, strove to avoid.

Table XV gives a comparison of mean Easter new moons, defined as above, and calendar Easter new moons at 19-year intervals from AD 1583 to AD 4414; it shows the march of the mean new moons and of the calendar new moons and the lag (L) of the latter behind the former, varying from zero to plus two days.

The initial mean Easter new moon of 1583 occurred on Mar 23.835432 and is computed from E. H. Lindo's results; he figured that a mean new moon occurred in AD 1845, October 1.654668,* from which date all other mean new moons can be computed by applying mean lunations of 29.530588 days. In this Table XV the work was carried out to six decimals, but only two are listed; they are sufficient for illustrative purposes.

A mean new moon in any given year is easily computed by subtracting 0.311820 of a day from the one that occurred 19 years earlier. For, if it is assumed that every 19-year period contains *five* intercalary days, it would contain $(19 \times 365 + 5)$ or 6940 days, which is 0.311820 of a day larger than (235×29.530588) or 6939.688180 days. Hence subtracting 0.311820 from a previous new moon date is equivalent to adding 235 mean lunations to it, the month and the day of the new moon remaining otherwise unchanged. It must be noted, however, that a 19-year period from the initial to the final new moon will contain only four intercalary days, if, 1°, the initial new moon falls in the last ten months of a year divisible by four, whether a leap year or not, or in the first two months of the year immediately following; or if, 2°, the 19-year period from initial to final new moon, loses an intercalary day in a century year not divisible by 400. In both these cases, therefore, the computer, as he proceeds, must supply these missing days, because the use of the subtrahend 0.311820 assumes that *every* 19-year period contains five intercalary days.

* Quoted in *Encyclopedia Britannica*, eleventh edition, *s. v. Calendar*. To this basic new moon date, and to all mean new moons derived from it, a correction might be applied, derived either from calendar considerations extending over a period of many thousands of years, or from a series of astronomical observations analyzed by means of the mathematical theory of the moon's motion; but Lindo's basic new moon date is sufficiently accurate for our purpose, and is here adopted.

For convenience in computing and tabulating, Apr 1 to Apr 5 are listed as Mar 32 to Mar 36.

A year's golden number determines its epact by Table IV, and the epact determines the calendar Easter new moon within its range of Mar 8 to Mar 36 (both included) by Table X.

The lag (L) is always taken in the sense: calendar new moon minus mean new moon.

A (4 × 19) or 76-year period may be used as a check on the correctness of the mean new moons in Table XV. For, since every such period ordinarily contains 19 intercalary days, it will contain (76 × 365 + 19) days; this will exceed (4 × 235) mean lunations by 0.247280 of a day. Hence, in any year a mean new moon may be derived from the one that occurred 76 years earlier by the use of this excess as subtrahend, the month and the day remaining otherwise unchanged; but the computer must supply the missing day whenever the 76-year period, from initial to final new moon, loses an intercalary day in a century year not divisible by 400. Any multiple of this 76-year interval, taken with its corresponding subtrahend, may be used in the same way; for instance, the interval of (76 × 24) or 1824 years with its subtrahend of (0.247280 × 24), or 5.934720 days.

Table XVI gives a similar comparison of *annual* Easter new moons, from 1928 to 2071. The initial mean new moon on Mar 21.854 was derived from the preceding Table; the work was carried to three decimals and controlled by the 19-year period.

A mean Easter new moon in any given year is derived from that of the preceding year by the addition of twelve or thirteen mean lunations and the subtraction of 365 or 366 days as the case may demand, according to the following Table.

Before Common Years		Before Leap Years	
12 × 29.530588 − 365 or −10.632944 (ordinary)	13 × 29.530588 − 365 or +18.897644 (embolismic)	12 × 29.530588 − 366 or −11.632944 (ordinary)	13 × 29.530588 − 366 or +17.897644 (embolismic)

In practice the operation is performed by applying one of the following four quantities to the preceding mean Easter new moon:

−10.633 +18.898 −11.633 +17.898

Any doubt as to when the embolismic terms are to be applied, must be solved by the *calendar* Easter new moon of the given year (see Table XVI).

Because of the neglected decimals, the results obtained should be corrected every nineteen years by means of the 19-year period with its subtrahend -0.311820 as explained above.

A mean new moon very rarely falls on the day *following* its calendar new moon, and then always before 6 A.M. of that day; it either coincides with, or precedes it by at most two days (plus a few hours at very rare intervals). There are no such exceptional cases in this and the preceding Table.

The 76-year period and its subtrahend 0.247280 is also useful for spanning long stretches of time; this may be illustrated by the solution of the important problem: On what day of the week was Passover in AD 33?

By adding 76-year periods to AD 33 one arrives at the year 1933, when by Table XVI the mean new moon preceding Easter, which in that year also ushered in the Passover lunation, because its fifteenth moon fell on or after Mar 26, occurred on Mar 26.750884 (unabbreviated decimals). Beginning with this mean new moon and working back, being careful to *add* 0.247280 every 76 years and to *subtract* one day when crossing a century year not divisible by 400, one arrives at Mar 17.93, for the Passover mean new moon in AD 33; this was Mar 18 according to the Jewish way of beginning the day at sundown of the preceding evening. If allowance is made for a possible day's lag of the computed, or of the observed new moon of this lunation behind the apparent new moon, the Passover new moon feast of AD 33 was celebrated on Mar 19. The fourteenth moon of that lunation (Nisan) occurred 13 days later on Apr 1, which was a Friday,* beginning on Thursday evening after sundown.

The present Jewish method of determining First Tishri and Passover, first published† by Hillel II, and adopted some time between AD 360 and 500, may be similarly carried back to the first century by means of the 76-year period, and puts Passover, or the fifteenth Nisan, of AD 33, on Apr 2, a Saturday.

This might well have been the year of the Crucifixion, for it agrees with what the Gospels imply. Christ celebrated the Passover (correctly) on Thursday evening (Matthew 26:20) when the Jewish Friday had already begun; whereas the Jews, following their paternal traditions, rejected Friday as a possible day for Passover, which they still do, and postponed the celebration to Saturday. Consequently, they would not enter Pilate's hall on Friday morning "that they might not be defiled, but that they might

* Friday, Apr 1 is a New Style date; contemporaries would have called this day Friday, Apr 3. Similarly, the New Style date Saturday, Apr 2, they would have called Saturday, Apr 4.

† *Jewish Encyclopedia, s. v. Calendar.*

eat the Passover" (John 18:28); Friday was the "Preparation of the Pasch" (John 19:14) and Saturday was a "*great* Sabbath" (John 19:31).

The six years immediately preceding AD 33 do not satisfy these details of the Passion, but AD 26 does. From calendar considerations, therefore, either AD 26 or 33, to the exclusion of the intervening years, might have been the year of Christ's death. The problem has an important bearing on the year of his birth and aptly illustrates calendar work in the service of history. (For further details, see *Appendix.*)

In all such problems the calendar correction of 1582 need not be regarded, and one may assume that the Gregorian Rule had been in force from the beginning of the Christian Era. Both the Christian, and the present Jewish calendar may correctly be projected into the remote past by means of the 76-year period. For, the sequence of the weeks has never been disturbed, neither were the Jewish new moons and yearly festivals changed by Hillel and his successors. But it must be remembered that the dates (month and day) thus derived are New Style dates and must be treated by means of New Style formulas and settings, to be explained later (*Section 31* and *Section 32*).

SECTION 23

General Remarks on the Gregorian Calendar

1° It is impossible to define Easter with reference to the true or apparent *full* moon. Easter is not necessarily the first Sunday after the first full moon that occurs on or after March 21—on or after the mean vernal equinox—on or after the beginning of spring.

2° Entire agreement must not be expected between the moons of the ecclesiastical calendar and the phases of the moon as listed in almanacs. In the latter, the true or apparent moon is used and allowance is made for all known irregularities in its motion; in the former, a conventional moon is adopted by using calendar moons, calendar lunations, even a calendar equinox.

For the sake of comparison the accompanying Table lists the true new moons for 1926 in Greenwich Civil Mean Time.* It clearly shows the variability of astronomical lunations, and the discrepancy between the calendar and astronomical new moon dates in that year.

3° In 1926 (GN = 8, Epact = XVI, DL is C) Easter was on Apr 4. The apparent Easter new moon on Mar 14 would have put the fourteenth moon of the Easter lunation on Mar 27, and Easter on Mar 28.

* Dates are taken from "The American Ephemeris and Nautical Almanac."

A similar postponement of Easter by one week takes place on the average about every fifth year. For, the calendar Easter new moon usually lags one or two days behind the mean Easter new moon, frequently resulting because of the dominical letter, in the celebration of Easter a week later than astronomical data would require.

The Church regards such discrepancy with perfect equanimity because, as Clavius blandly remarks, she cares more for peace and uniformity than she does for the equinox and the new moon. That discrepancy is not unintentional; it is the price that the Church has to pay to keep Easter from preceding or coinciding with Passover.

AD 1926

Calendar New Moons	True New Moons	True Lunations
Jan 15	Jan 14.27	29.45
Feb 13	Feb 12.72	29.42
Mar 15	Mar 14.14	29.40 (m)
Apr 13	Apr 12.54	29.42
May 13	May 11.96	29.47
Jun 11	Jun 10.42	29.54
Jul 11	Jul 9.96	29.61
Aug 9	Aug 8.58	29.66
Sep 8	Sep 7.24	29.69 (M)
Oct 7	Oct 6.93	29.68
Nov 6	Nov 5.61	29.65
Dec 5	Dec 5.26	

The Jews, too, in their former observation of the Passover new moon naturally had a similar lag; and in their present method of computing their Passover date, they frequently have a lag of one whole lunation, since they do not regard a full moon occurring prior to Mar 26 as the Passover date, but celebrate the feast one lunation later. In such years the Church does not accommodate herself to the practice of the Synagogue. Evidently, in devising their present method of determining the First of Tishri and from it the date of the preceding Passover, the Jews had regard to a pre-Christian century when the equivalent of our March 26* was the beginning of spring.

4° Every calendar whether solar or lunar, must to some extent be conventional, and therefore arbitrary, since it is designed to measure time by an integral number of units to the exclusion of decimals. The year and the

* This would indicate BC 300 to 200 as the beginning of their present method of computing 1 Tishri, and would mean that about 200 years after Meton's time, the Jews under Greek influence adopted the Metonic cycle, and began to apply *mean* lunations to some basic autumnal mean new moon date.

day, natural solar units, are incommensurable; likewise the lunation and the day, natural lunar units. The true lunation is variable, due to the perturbations of the moon and the earth in their orbits; the tropical year, from the true equinox to the true equinox, is variable, due to the perturbations of the earth. The true vernal equinox is therefore not a suitable anchorage for a calendar.

All that can be reasonably required of any calendar is that, of the many possible ways of measuring time, the one chosen shall satisfy *all* the requirements of the problem at hand, and while doing so, shall be as simple as possible. The Christian luni-solar calendar with its Gregorian corrections satisfies this requirement. No better working substitute, meeting all the conditions of the problem, has ever been found.

5° Of the Christian calendar, especially its lunar part as modified by the Gregorian reform, the explanation is unavoidably complicated; but the application—golden number, epact, dominical letter, Easter—is remarkably simple. The few tables required are always available in the Roman Missal or Breviary.

6° One who suggests substituting the astronomical equinox and lunations instead of the calendar equinox and calendar new moons to compute the Easter date, should be challenged to find Easter, for instance, of the year 432, or of the year 4178 by his proposed method, or to compute a few scattered Passovers in the Jewish way (see *Appendix*), and he will begin to realize the extraordinary simplicity of the Christian luni-solar calendar with its Gregorian improvements.

It was precisely such a substitution of astronomical lunar tables, that was attempted by the Protestant States of Germany in 1700, and again by the atheistic government during the French Revolution; in both attempts the substitution was soon found impracticable and was abandoned; for it required very extensive lunar tables, possessed and understood by few, and it sometimes determined Easters at variance with those observed by other Christian nations. An astronomical definition of Easter is, as we have seen, impossible.

Section 24

Future Corrections to the Gregorian Solar Calendar

In 1582 a mean tropical year of 365.2425 days was adopted. (*Section 4.*) If we take 365 days, 5 hours, 48 minutes, 46.1 seconds, or 365.2422 days as the mean tropical year—a value correct to five decimals—the annual correction needed by the Gregorian solar calendar is (365.2422 − 365.2425) or -0.0003 days. This will amount to (-0.0003×3200) or -0.96 of a day every 3200 years. If the last year of that general interval were a leap year, and were to be reduced to a common year by the subtraction of one whole day, the correction would then be $+0.04$ days.

After (25×3200) or 80,000 years, the correction needed would be $(+0.04 \times 25)$, or exactly $+1$ day. If, then, the common year at the end of this interval were to receive an additional day and be restored as a leap year, the process could begin anew. Instead of the 400-year period obtained in *Section 4*, 80,000 years would be an *exact repeating unit* of solar time.

To express these general intervals in terms of the Christian Era, and to make these corrections applicable in century leap years, we assume that the solar calendar was correctly adjusted for AD 1600—the 18 years from 1582 to 1600 with a correction of (-0.0003×18), or less than 8 minutes, being negligible. The year $(1600 + 3200)$, or AD 4800, though a multiple of 400, would then be a century common year; likewise the years AD 8000, 11,200 etc. But the year $(1600 + 80{,}000)$, or AD 81,600 would again be a century leap year.

The common years supplanting Gregorian leap years would have to be reflected by solar equations in the lunar calendar (Table III), because the only way to subtract one day from the lunar calendar without disturbing the lunar tables is to apply the solar equation; and the series of epacts (Table IV) would be affected, beginning with AD 4800.

An interval of 4000 years, and multiples thereof, has been suggested instead of 3200 years. The proposal is objectionable for the following reason.

The yearly correction of -0.0003 would amount to (-0.0003×4000), or -1.2 days at the end of every 4,000 years. Reducing the last year of this interval, in the assumption that it is a leap year, would leave as correction -0.2 days. After five such intervals, or 20,000 years, the correction needed would be minus one day. Now the last year of that interval would already be a common year as a multiple of 4,000; applying to it the further correction of minus one day would make it an *incomplete* year of 364 days. The same thing would happen at the end of every multiple of the 20,000-year interval. But there is no provision for a 364-day year in the calendar. The last correction could, indeed, be applied four years before or after the end of the interval, but that would be inelegant.

It would be preferable to make AD 3200 and multiples thereof common years; but to retain the year (25×3200) or AD 80,000 and multiples thereof as leap years. This would apply the corrective *whole* day as often as the error of the present solar calendar reaches one half-day, three half-days, five half-days, etc.

Section 25

Future Corrections to the Gregorian Lunar Calendar

If the mean astronomical lunation is taken as 29.530588 days, which is the best value known to date, the correction required by the lunar calendar, applicable to the epacts, every 19 years, is +0.06182 days. (*Section 10.*) This will amount to $\left(\frac{+0.06182}{19} \times 2500\right)$, or +8.13421 days every 2500 years. The reformers applied the eight whole days as lunar equations to every such interval, leaving a correction of +0.13421 days needed by the lunar calendar every 2500 years.

After (8 × 2500), or 20,000 years, this will amount to (+0.13421 × 8) or +1.07368 days, and would require an *additional* lunar equation of +1 day every 20,000 years, leaving a correction of +0.07368 days.

After (14 × 20,000) or 280,000 years, this would amount to (+0.07368 × 14) or +1.03152 days, again requiring an *additional* lunar equation of +1 day every 280,000 years, leaving a correction of +0.03152 days, and so forth.

Hence, if we begin these general intervals with AD 1800, thereby neglecting a small correction of less than 17 minutes for the 218 years from 1582 to 1800, the year (1800 + 20,000) or AD 21,800, and the years 41,800, 61,800, etc., would each require a lunar equation of +2 days; and the years AD 281,800, 561,800, etc., would each require a lunar equation of +3 days in Table III, affecting the series of epacts in Table IV.

The Gregorian lunar calendar is, therefore, far more accurate than its solar counterpart. The former clock will run 20,000 years before it needs adjusting; the latter clock will run only 3200 years.

At the time of the calendar reform, the mean lunation was known with greater accuracy than the mean solar year. This is not surprising. The astronomical new moon can be observed rather well without instruments; there are 12 or 13 of them to the year, and for religious reasons, they had been observed for many centuries; whereas the beginning of the solar year is not immediately observable, and never had the same religious interest as the new moons. The accurate observation of eclipses could begin only after the invention of the telescope and of the pendulum clock.

Section 26

A Suggested Improvement Regarding the Intercalary Day

The Church inherited the fictitious 48-hour day for Feb 24 in leap years (*Section 21*) from pagan times. In the ancient Roman calendar this double day in leap years was *twice* designated as *a.d. VI Kal. Mart.*,* whence it was called "dies bissextilis," and the leap year got the name "annus bissextilis."

For her purpose, Feb 28 as a 48-hour day, the first half to be intercalary, would serve as well as Feb 24; and the change would bring the ecclesiastical solar calendar nearer to the present civil calendar, and it would make four days, now vacant, available for annual festivals of Saints. Feb 28 could then be called "dies bispridialis," and the leap year an "annus bispridialis," from the Roman date, *Pridie Kal. Mart.* (= eve of Mar 1). This would require a slight change in the lists of Saints' festivals—the transfer of the feast of St. Matthias from Feb 24 to Feb 28.

But the Catholic Church is very tenacious of the customs of the past and changes them only for the gravest of reasons; that is why she adopts a hesitant attitude towards proposed new civil calendars.

Section 27

Proposed New Civil Calendars

The variability of the present yearly civil calendar, due to the fact that the year does not contain an exact number of weeks, has suggested a change in its structure.

The objections to the present yearly calendar are mainly these:

1° Successive years are not comparable with one another. Some years are leap years, others common; some contain 53 Sundays, others only 52, with the consequent difference in the number of business or working days in each.

2° The months are not comparable; one month may contain 27 business days, and the very next one only 24. While this variability is of little consequence in agriculture and small trades, its effects are disturbing in large manufacturing corporations, and merchandising concerns, where the pay-rolls, income, etc., fluctuate considerably on this account from month to month.

3° The Easter trade in some years swells the March receipts; in others, the April receipts.

4° Successive years begin with different days of the week requiring wall- or desk-calendars renewable every year, and without which it is impossible to know on what day of the week a certain date falls.

* *Ante diem sextum Kalendas Martias*, means "the sixth day referred to the coming Martian Kalends."

In subtracting, moderns exclude the first term, thus, in common years, Feb 24 to Mar 1 is five days. The ancients did not subtract; they added and included both extremes, thus Feb 24 was the sixth day to Mar 1.

To overcome these difficulties the following are the two principal schemes (with minor variations) that have been proposed:

1° Let every year begin on a Sunday and be divided into 13 months of 28 days each. Let the last day of the year, and in leap years, the last day of the second month be a 48-hour Saturday—the last half of such a double Saturday to be a holiday. All months will be comparable and have the same number (24) of business or working days. The first, eighth, fifteenth, and twenty-second day of every month will be a Sunday, thus enabling one to compute the days mentally without the use of wall-calendars. Finally let the Easter and Passover festivals be assigned to fixed days of the solar year.

2° The second scheme is like the first, except that it retains the present 12 months, but it introduces a change in the number of days in these months. Every quarter is to have two months of 30 days each, and one month of 31 days. All quarters would begin on a Sunday and end on Saturday, and would be comparable with one another; but the months within the quarters would not be comparable as to the number of business days in each.* The year would end with a 48-hour Saturday; before leap years, according to some, there would be a triple Saturday (72 hours); according to others the second month of the leap year would end with a double Wednesday; according to others, the second quarter in a leap year would end with a double Saturday.

The great objection to all such proposals is that they interrupt the sequence of the weeks at least once every year; this seems to be an insurmountable difficulty for religious reasons.

From their very beginning as a people, the Hebrews observed every seventh day as a day of rest, because God "rested on the seventh day and blessed it and sanctified it." (Genesis 2:2.) Later He commanded them: "Remember that thou keep holy the rest day." (Exodus 20:8.) The day of Passover too was prescribed by the divine Lawgiver (Leviticus 23:5) according to the lunar, not to the solar calendar. It is difficult to see by what authority present-day Jews could sanction a yearly interruption of the Sabbaths and the fixation of Passover to a specified day of the solar year.

The Mohammedans would object to the yearly interruption of their weekly holy days (Fridays).

The Catholic Church in apostolic times exercised the plenitude of power granted her by her divine Founder (Matthew 16:19), and in honor of the Resurrection substituted the Lord's Day for the Jewish Sabbath; but the sequence of the weeks was not thereby interrupted. It is one thing to

* If, however, the 31-day month were placed at the beginning of its quarter, the months would not be comparable in the number of their weekly paydays.

change once and for all a Levitical ceremonial law for grave reasons, and quite another thing to allow apostolic traditions to be interfered with once every year or oftener. For this reason the "decades" decreed during the French Revolution were not approved; Catholics continued to keep their Sundays as of old.

And why should this momentous change be made? As a matter of convenience in accountancy! Almost the whole civilized world—Christian, Jewish, Moslem—is asked to alter its religious observances every year in order that one monthly or quarterly report may be comparable with another. The national holidays of all countries are to be re-allocated, not according to historical dates, but to suit the convenience of business life. Surely our public accountants are not so unskilled in their art that they cannot solve their own problems in another way. Let them work with 28-day periods, if they will; let them count only business or working days; let them standardize their results by means of conversion factors; but let them not ask the whole world to adapt itself to their needs. Even if Easter and Passover were stabilized, the Easter trade, like the Christmas trade, would still be seasonal, unless, perhaps, they propose to do something about the weather!

Should, however, a change in the yearly civil calendar be decided on, there is only one proposed plan that deserves to be characterized as scientific. Radical as it may seem, the 13-month year is the only one that would be worth the trouble entailed in its introduction; the others are compromises of less value.

Section 28

A Universal Paschal Table Without Epacts

To avoid the use of epacts, so baffling to most people, we have reverted to the method of the ancients (*Section 17*) and constructed a new paschal table, by which the movable feasts, both before and after 1582, can be found from a given year's golden number and dominical letter, without the use of any epacts (Table XVIII).

This universal paschal table is used as follows: Compute the GN and the DL for the given year. (*Section 2* and *Section 3.*) In the column of Table XVIII proper to the period, find the current GN; then the current DL next *below* that line indicates the civil dates of the movable feasts.

Example 1: Find Easter in AD 1450.

We have: GN = 7, DL is D

The number 7 in the first column of Table XVIII determines the line; the first D *below* that line points to Apr 5 as Easter.

Example 2: Find the movable feasts in AD 1916.

We have: GN = 17, DL is BA—a leap year.

The number 17 in the fourth column determines the line; the next A *below* that line puts Septuagesima on Feb (19 + 1) or Feb 20, Ash Wednesday on Mar 8, Easter on Apr 23, etc.

Example 3: Find Easter in AD 3398 using Table XVIII; and again using Table IV and Table X or Table XI. Which method is simpler?

Answer: Easter on Mar 25; the former method is simpler because it requires the use of only *one* table, and uses the familiar golden numbers instead of the strange epacts.

In a leap year whose golden number stands at the end of its column, and whose dominical letters are DC, the same caution is necessary as that given at the end of *Section 15*; for example, in finding Septuagesima in AD 672 (GN = 8, DL is DC) the use of D would put this Sunday on the wrong date, Feb 15 instead of Feb 22.

This universal paschal table may be constructed by substituting for the epacts in Table X, their corresponding golden numbers taken from Table IV for the various periods. It may also be derived directly from the golden numbers without the use or knowledge of epacts; this we now proceed to do.

There are two ways to apply a correction to the lunar calendar:

1° The first method keeps the yearly calendar, and the paschal table derived from it, *intact*, and applies the correction to the current series of epacts in Table IV, giving rise to a new series of epacts. This is the method that we are familiar with and use whenever a solar or lunar equation is to be applied.

2° The second method would raise the whole column of epacts in the yearly calendar and in its derived paschal table by the number of lines corresponding to a lunar equation, and lower the column of epacts by the number of lines corresponding to a solar equation. This method, unfamiliar to us, was used in 1582 to restore the epacts to their original definition; it has never been used since, because it changes the yearly calendar and derived paschal table.

This is the method that we now apply, not to the yearly calendar, which is left intact, but to a *new* paschal table to be derived from it; not to the epacts which are entirely disregarded, but to the column of the golden numbers.

Elevating the golden number column against the calendar dates applies a lunar equation, and lowering the column applies a solar equation.

To realize this fact, consider the Old Style yearly calendar (Table XIII), in which the golden numbers used to indicate the new moon dates. Thus, a year whose GN = 11 would have the new moons on Mar 3, Apr 2, May 1, etc. Raising the golden number column one line against the calendar dates, diminishes the new moon dates by one day; this is precisely what the lunar equation does through the epacts in the reformed calendar. (See *Section 10.*) Lowering the column one line augments the new moon dates, which is precisely what the solar equation does through the epacts in the reformed calendar. (See *Section 9.*)

Construction of the universal paschal table

From the Old Style yearly calendar (Table XIII), the golden number column beginning with 16, 5, etc., properly spaced, corresponding to the range of the Easter new moons, Mar 8 to Apr 5 (both included) is copied unchanged in column A of Table XVII, for use to 1582.

In that year three days were added to the lunar calendar by aligning the asterisk ✳ with Jan 1, and ten days were subtracted from it through the epacts; effectively, therefore, seven days were subtracted.

The golden numbers of column A are therefore lowered seven lines in column B, and the upper part of the column is replenished with golden numbers, properly spaced, preceding Mar 8 in the old yearly calendar; column B is for use from 1583 to 1699.

In 1700, 1900, 2200, 2300, each of the solar equations effective in those years (see Table III) requires the further lowering of the golden number column one line, as shown in column C, D, E, F.

In 2400 the effective lunar equation requires the raising of the golden number column one line, as shown in column M, and so forth.

It must be noted that, whereas the range of the Easter new moon dates, Mar 8 to Apr 5, contains only 29 dates, the various columns in Table XVII must contain 30 lines each; for each column must contain all 19 golden numbers, and if it had only 29 lines, it would often happen that, when the last golden number at the bottom of a column passed beyond the range, a vacant space would enter the column at the top, instead of the golden number that left the range below.

One of these 30 lines, barring the first and the last, can and must be eliminated. In order that the universal paschal table that is to result may conform to the New Style yearly calendar, the paschal tables, and the results derived from them, we choose to clear the second last line by lowering its single golden numbers to the last line, and where this is impossible, by raising them to the Apr 4 line. This raising of any golden number to the higher line always takes place in a period when in epact tables [25] is used instead of XXV. The last line, now fully stocked with golden numbers, is attributed to Apr 5.

It is to be noted further that columns M and N, identical with E and F respectively, may be omitted and otherwise provided for. The further omission of the Easter new moon dates, and the addition of the dominical letters, corresponding to the range of the fourteenth moon of the Easter lunation (Mar 21 to Apr 18 and beyond), supplemented by the civil list of movable feasts, results in the new universal paschal table (XVIII); it may be extended indefinitely.

Section 29

Annual Martyrology Letters

The Martyrology letter (ML) for any given year can be determined by means of the year's golden number without the use of any epacts. For this purpose Table XIX has been constructed, to be used as follows: The given year's golden number, in the column proper to the period, is always found on the same line as the year's martyrology letter.

Examples. Find the ML for the following years:

(1) 1940. We have: GN = 3 (by *Section 2*). In the sixth column headed 1900–2199, the number 3 determines the line on which is found in the last column, ML is B.
(2) 1944. GN = 7, Answer: ML is e
(3) 2516. 9 F
(4) 2926. 1 F
(5) 1954. 17 [F] applied directly to 17
(6) 3108. 12 [F] " " " 12
(7) 876. 3 a

The meaning of this last result is: In the present Martyrology in use since issued by Pope Gregory XIII, in 1584, as a part of the Gregorian Reform, the letter "a" will indicate the moon's age that had to be announced in choir every day during the year 876.

Construction of Table XIX

This new table contains in the last column the repeating series of 30 letters, given in *Section 14*; but they are conveniently written in reverse order. The letter [F] is omitted from the series and applied directly to the proper golden number in the period when it occurs.

The series of golden numbers 16, 5, 13, 2, etc., properly spaced, is taken from the Old Style yearly calendar (Table XIII) and one of its numbers, for instance, 16, in the column headed 1582–1699, is alined with the letter r. This position of 16 is required in this period, because the golden number 16 corresponded to the epact XVI (Table IV), and the epact XVI is represented by the Martyrology letter r. (*Section 14.*) This fixes the position of the whole system of golden numbers in Table XIX.

Before 1582 only 19 letters of the alphabet were used to represent the golden numbers (or the traditional epacts); they are the 19 small letters of the series still in use. About once every 300 years it had been found necessary to apply the equivalent of a lunar equation in order to keep the moon's age, as announced in choir, in rough agreement with the observed phases of the moon. The necessity of solar equations went unnoticed for many centuries, because their omission affected only the calendar date of the beginning of spring—an occurrence not so readily observable as the daily age of the moon.

The application of this lunar correction did not affect the 19-year cycle (Table XII), nor the yearly calendar (Table XIII), nor the paschal table (XIV); all these three Old Style tables remained unchanged. The lunar correction was applied directly to the series of 19 letters then in use, by lowering the whole series of letters one line against the repeating series of golden numbers (or traditional epacts); this was done in the years 320, 500, 800, 1100, and 1400. In Table XIX the *letters* are stationary, hence the series of golden numbers must be raised one line every time a lunar equation is applied.

In 1582, the correction of ten days applied to the solar calendar entailed the lowering of the golden number series *fully* ten lines in this table—not seven lines as in Table XVIII—because the series of 30 letters is here assumed to remain *unchanged*, and the correction of ten days was not partially counteracted as in Table XVIII, by the raising of the golden number and epact columns of the Old Style yearly calendar three lines. (See *Section 18.*)

Since 1582 the various periods, determined by the application of solar and lunar equations, are treated as in Table XVIII.

In *practice*, therefore, no knowledge of epacts is necessary. Table XVIII and Table XIX, used with a given year's computed golden number and dominical letter, afford all the required data for that year in the simplest possible way. By means of them the list of such data from 1941 to 1980, given in Table XX, was composed. Both tables can easily be extended to embrace any later centuries.

The *theory* of epacts is, however, needed in constructing Table XIX;

first, for the choice of 30, instead of the old 19 letters in the last column; then, to adapt the whole system of golden numbers to the fixed series of those 30 letters; and finally, to determine the periods when [F] must be used instead of F.

Were one willing to omit the letter-number scheme in the Martyrology and to forego announcing the daily age of the moon at the hour of Prime in choir, the whole complicated machinery of the epacts, with its lengthy explanations and numerous tables, could be scrapped; it would not be missed. The golden numbers, limited though they are, would suffice to explain and apply the entire lunar part of the calendar.

Section 30

A Simplified Luni-solar Christian Calendar

It will now be shown how, if the necessity of using Martyrology letters were dispensed with, the Gregorian Calendar could be greatly simplified; for the theory and use of epacts could be entirely avoided, the whole calendar explained, and its few necessary tables derived by means of the golden numbers. The following is an outline of the necessary steps.

First step. The Old Style 19-year cycle of new moon dates (Table XII) is constructed, bearing golden numbers only. The conditions for placing the seven half-days are: 1° The lunation current at the year's end must always contain 30 days. 2° There must be no duplicate new moon dates. 3° In years whose golden numbers are 3, 8, 11, or 19, the half-days must be shifted from the end of the year to the first complete lunation. The reason for these conditions is here a practical one; namely, that the results to be obtained from this table may agree with those derived from the historical OS and NS yearly calendars and lunar tables.

Second step. The Old Style yearly calendar (Table XIII), bearing golden numbers only, is constructed—the year beginning Mar 1. It is then to be shown how a year's golden number indicates the new moon dates of that year in the calendar; how, in case it should ever become necessary to raise or lower the golden number column, *all* the calendar dates become new moon dates; how raising the golden number column diminishes the new moon dates, and lowering the column augments the new moon dates of the calendar.

Third step. It is next to be shown how the excessive length of Meton's lunar yardstick requires that the new moon dates be diminished by eight days every 2500 years, for after every 307 years it indicates new moon dates that are each one day too large, thus requiring that the golden number column be raised one line; also, how the omission of an intercalary day in the solar calendar requires that the new moon dates be augmented, for when the very next new moon occurs it finds the day called, for instance, Mar 2 instead of Mar 1, thus requiring that the golden number column be lowered one line.

Table III is next constructed containing lunar and solar equations, but no epacts. The algebraic sign of these equations must be changed, for they are now applied, not to the epacts, but directly to the new moon dates; the corresponding raising or lowering of the golden number column is not done in the Old Style yearly calendar itself, but in a universal paschal table to be derived from it.

Fourth step. From the Old Style yearly calendar (Table XIII) the golden numbers within the Easter new moon range (Mar 8 to Apr 5) are transferred, properly spaced, to a universal paschal table (Table XVIII), whose construction is described in *Section 28*. In 1582 the calendar dates (= new moon dates) were augmented by ten days by omitting Oct 5 to Oct 14, requiring the golden number column to be lowered ten lines; but at the same time the calendar dates were diminished by three days, because of the epacts, requiring the golden number column to be raised three lines. Effectively therefore the column had to be lowered *seven* lines, etc.

Fifth step. The New Style yearly calendar (Table IX) is then independently constructed, bearing the dominical letters, but not epacts or golden numbers—the year beginning Jan 1. It is exactly like a civil calendar but lacks Feb 29 in leap years. The 48-hour day in Feb is then explained as in *Section 21*, showing how the intercalary day is accounted for without altering the yearly calendar.

Thus five tables would be required; all the other tables would be superfluous. The results would be identical with those found by means of epacts both before and after 1582.

Section 31

An Adjustable Yearly Calendar

It will be very useful to have a civil calendar that can be easily adjusted for any given year of the Christian Era. Such a perpetual yearly calendar is attached to the cover at the end of this book.

On the movable part or *insert* is printed an ordinary yearly calendar without the customary designation of the days of the week. It is a common year calendar, but it bears the date Feb 29 for use in leap years, without however interrupting the common year sequence of the dates, Feb 28, Mar 1. The dominical letters are conveniently placed below, as shown, for the purpose of adjusting the calendar.

The transparent *jacket*, attached to the book cover, has printed above a continuous line of abbreviations for the days of the week, and an index below, all properly spaced and located to agree with the printed calendar on the insert.

This new perpetual calendar is adjusted for use as follows: For any given year of the Christian Era, the year beginning on Jan 1, the dominical letter is found either by the formulas given in *Section 3*, or by Table I. This current dominical letter on the movable insert is then alined with the fixed index on the jacket, and the calendar is ready for use.

Since leap years have two dominical letters, two settings of the calendar are required for such years, one for Jan–Feb dates, and another for Mar–Dec dates.

The calendar may also be adjusted without regard to the dominical letters; a given year's dominical number found by formula may be directly used for this purpose, in combination with the first seven dates in January. For example, suppose that a common year's dominical number has been found to be 4; this means that Jan 4 is a Sunday, since the dominical numbers, like the dominical letters, begin with Jan 1 (*Section 3*). Set the calendar so that Jan 4 coincides with a Sunday. In a leap year *both* settings are effected in the same way by the use of the first seven dates in January.

Both in its construction and in its use, the adjustable calendar is independent of any conversion constants; for, the dominical letter needed may be found by the use of Table I, in whose construction or proof such constants did not necessarily enter.

For convenience, the formulas of *Section 3* are here repeated:

$$\text{For OS years: DN} = 10 - \left(6\text{ H} + \text{Y} + \frac{\text{Y}}{4}\right)$$

$$\text{For NS years: DN} = 8 - \left(5\text{ H} + \frac{\text{H}}{4} + \text{Y} + \frac{\text{Y}}{4}\right)$$

(the year being first reduced to a Jan 1 year.)

Example 1. Adjust the calendar for AD 857.

This is an OS common year; hence,

by formula: DN $= 10 - (6 + 1 + 0)$ or 3; DL is C;
or by Table I: 857 $\div$ 28 leaves R $= 17$; T $= 0$; DL is C.
Bringing C of the adjustable calendar to the index, one sees that Jan 1, 857 fell on Friday, etc.

Example 2. Adjust the calendar for AD 1492.

This is an OS leap year.

By formula: DN $= 10 - (0 + 1 + 2) = 7$; DL is AG;
or by Table I: 1492 $\div$ 28 leaves R $= 8$; T $= 0$; DL is AG.

Bring A to the index for Jan–Feb dates.	Jan 1, 1492	fell on	Sunday
	Feb. 29, 1492	" "	Wednesday
Bring G to the index for Mar–Dec dates.	Mar 1, 1492	" "	Thursday
	Oct 12, 1492	" "	Friday,

the day on which Columbus discovered America.

Example 3. Adjust the calendar for AD 1900.

This is a NS *common* year!

By formula: DN $= 8 - (4 + 4 + 0 + 0)$ or 7; DL is G;
or by Table I: 1900 $\div$ 28 leaves R $= 24$; T $= 24$; R $+$ T $- 28 = 20$; and DL is G (for the *whole* year).
Bring G to the index. Jan 1, 1900 fell on Monday, etc.

Example 4. Adjust the calendar for AD 1992.

This is a NS leap year.

By formula: DN $= 8 - (4 + 4 + 1 + 2)$ or 4; DL is ED;
or by Table I: 1992 $\div$ 28 leaves R $= 4$; T $= 12$; R $+$ T $= 16$; DL is ED.
Bring E to the index. Feb 29, 1992 will fall on Saturday.
" D " " " Dec 31, 1992 " " " Thursday

Example 5. Adjust the calendar for AD 1582.

Because of the Calendar Reform in this year, two settings of the calendar are needed: one for Jan 1 to Oct 4, another for Oct 15 to Dec 31.

(1) For dates from Jan 1 to Oct 4.
By OS formula: DN $= 10 - (6 + 5 + 6)$ or 7; DL is G;
or by Table I: 1582 $\div$ 28 leaves R $= 14$; T $= 0$; DL is G.
Bring G to the index. Oct 4, 1582 fell on Thursday.

(2) For dates from Oct 15 to Dec 31.
By NS formula: DN $= 8 - (5 + 3 + 5 + 6)$ or 3; DL is C;
or by Table I: 1582 $\div$ 28 leaves R $= 14$; T $= 20$; R $+$ T $- 28 = 6$; DL is C.

Bring C to the index. Oct 15, 1582 fell on Friday.
The ten dates Oct 5 to Oct 14 were omitted from the calendar and Thu, Oct 4, 1582 was immediately followed by Fri, Oct 15.

Example 6. Adjust the calendar for AD 0.

This was an OS *leap* year. Hence,
by formula: DN = 10 − (0 + 0 + 0) or 3; DL is DC;
or by Table I: 0 ÷ 28 leaves R = 0; T = 0; R + T = 0; DL is DC.
Bring D to the index. Jan 1 of AD 0 was Thursday—the first day of the Christian Era, if that year is first reduced to a year beginning on Jan 1, as is here assumed.
Bring C to the index. Mar 1 of AD 0 was Monday.

Section 32

Formulas to Find the Day of the Week for a Given Date

THE DAY of the week on which a given date falls, may be directly computed by a new formula, without the use of any table or calendar. The given date is first reduced, when necessary, to a year beginning with Jan 1. The formula then has the general form:

$$D_W = E_Y + E_M + E_D + \text{a constant.}$$

These symbols are now to be explained.

D_W is the number of the given day in its week; Sunday being 1, Monday, 2, etc.

E_Y is the excess over the highest multiple of seven with which the given year begins; it is found by means of the polynomials derived in *Section 3*.

Hence,

$$E_Y = \begin{cases} 6\,H + Y + \dfrac{Y}{4} & \text{in OS years.} \\[2ex] 5\,H + \dfrac{H}{4} + Y + \dfrac{Y}{4} & \text{in NS years.} \end{cases}$$

E_M is the excess, accumulated in its year, with which the given month (M) begins; E_M is found, either by writing the preceding (M − 1) months, each with its excess over 28 days, when the sum of these partial excesses will be E_M; or, for dates after February, it may be found by the formula:

$$E_M = 3\,(M - 2) - N_{30} + 1_L$$

where M is the number of the given month in its year, January being 1, February being 2, etc; N_{30} is the number of 30-day months *preceding* M; 1_L is unity, to be added in leap years only.

The proof of this formula for E_M is easy. If every month had 31 days, 28 days of each could be dropped, and (M − 1) months would contain 3 (M − 1) excessive days; from this must be subtracted three days for February in common years (two days only in leap years), and one day each for the N 30-day months preceding M.

Hence, $E_M = 3\,(M - 1) - 3 - N_{30} + 1_L$

or $= 3\,(M - 2) - N_{30} + 1_L$ Q. e. d.

E_D is the excess of the given date in its month; thus for Mar 25, E_D is (25 − 21) or 4.

The constant is called "conversion constant" because it is a number that will convert the total excess of a given date into the corresponding day of the week. This constant will have one of four values: P for OS leap years, Q for OS common years, R for NS leap years, S for NS common years. Q and S have already been determined from two known common year dates in *Section 3*, where it was found that

$$Q = 5$$
$$S = 7 \text{ or } 0.$$

P is found from a known OS leap year date, for instance Friday, Oct 12, 1492, on which day America was discovered.

Hence, $6 = (0 + 1 + 2) + 1 + 5 + P$

and therefore $P = 4$

R is found from a NS leap year date, such as Sunday, Aug 11, 1940.

Hence, $1 = (4 + 4 + 5 + 3) + 3 + 4 + R$

and therefore $R = 6$

Substituting these results in the general formula given above, one obtains the forms most easily applied in practice:

$$D_W = \left(6\,H + Y + \frac{Y}{4}\right) + E_M + E_D + \begin{cases} 4 \text{ in OS leap years} \\ 5 \text{ in OS common years} \end{cases} \qquad \text{I}$$

$$D_W = \left(5\,H + \frac{H}{4} + Y + \frac{Y}{4}\right) + E_M + E_D + \begin{cases} 6 \text{ in NS leap years} \\ 7 \text{ in NS common years} \end{cases} \qquad \text{II}$$

The constants 4, 5, 6, and 7 are easily remembered.

These two formulas assume that the year began on January 1; hence OS dates must first be reduced to a Jan 1st year. This is easily done by adding one unit to the number of the given OS year for all dates between Jan 1 and the beginning of the following OS year; other dates remain unchanged.

Thus, Feb 15, 1432 (Mar 1st year) was Feb 15, 1433 (Jan 1st year). Another formula for finding the day of the week on which a given date falls, requires *all* dates to be first reduced to a Mar 1st year, which is confusing in practice.

Some examples will illustrate the use of the formula:

Example 1. What day of the week was AD 0, Jan 1; Mar 1; Mar 25?

AD 0 was an OS *leap* year. (*Section 1.*)

By formula:

$D_W = (0 + 0 + 0) + 0 + 1 + 4$ *Ans.* Jan 1 was 5, Thursday.
$D_W = (0 + 0 + 0) + 4 + 1 + 4$ Mar 1 was 2, Monday.
$D_W = (0 + 0 + 0) + 4 + 4 + 4$ Mar 25 was 5, Thursday.

Find these same dates by means of the adjustable civil calendar.

Example 2. What day of the week was AD 1, Jan 1; Mar 1; Mar 25?

This was an OS common year.

By formula:

$D_W = (0 + 1 + 0) + 0 + 1 + 5$ *Ans.* Jan 1 was 7, Saturday.
$D_W = (0 + 1 + 0) + 3 + 1 + 5$ Mar 1 was 3, Tuesday.
$D_W = (0 + 1 + 0) + 3 + 4 + 5$ Mar 25 was 6, Friday.

Again use the adjustable civil calendar to obtain these same results.

Example 3. What day of the week was AD 326, Apr 3?

This was an OS common year.

$D_W = (4 + 5 + 6) + 6 + 3 + 5$ *Ans.* 1, Sunday.

Show that it was Easter Sunday. *Ans.* GN = 4, DL is B, use Table XVIII.

Example 4. What day of the week was AD 1600, Feb 29?

This was a NS leap year

$D_W = (3 + 4 + 0 + 0) + 3 + 1 + 6$ *Ans.* 3, Tuesday.

The dominical letters for this year are BA. Find the same result using B with the part of the civil calendar given in *Section 21*. Again, using A with the ecclesiastical calendar in Table IX. (Read *Section 21.*)

Example 5. What day of the week will AD 2100, July 4 be?

This is a NS *common* year. (*Section 4.*)

$D = (0 + 5 + 0 + 0) + 6 + 4 + 7$ *Ans.* 1, Sunday.

It must be noted that the Old Style year began on various dates according to country and period. It is now the universal custom for writers to give the *year* of an OS historical date in NS (Jan 1st year), retaining the OS month and day; such dates are said to be "partially corrected." Old monuments, however, tombstones, contemporary documents, etc., contain uncorrected OS dates. Such dates cannot be corrected, even partially, unless one knows when the year began in that particular place and time, and when the Gregorian Reform was introduced in that locality—data obtainable as a rule only from special works on chronology.

In *England* and her colonies, the Gregorian Reform was adopted in 1752; Wednesday, Sep 2 being immediately followed by Thursday Sep 14. From the year 1155 on, the English year had begun on Mar 25. Hence uncorrected OS English dates within the interval 1155 to 1752 are partially corrected or reduced to a year beginning Jan 1, by *adding* one unit to the year for Jan 1 to Mar 24 dates; for Mar 25 to Dec 31 dates no correction is needed.

Example 6. A textbook records the death of Mary, Queen of Scots, as of 1587, Feb 8. What day of the week was that?

This is an OS "partially corrected" date (Jan 1st year).

$D_W = (6 + 3 + 0) + 3 + 1 + 5$ *Ans.* 4, Wednesday.

Example 7. On what day of the week was George Washington born? The baptismal record reads 1731, Feb 11.

This is an OS uncorrected date; it was 1732, Feb 11 (Jan 1st year), a *leap* year.

$D_W = (4 + 4 + 1) + 3 + 4 + 4$ *Ans.* 6, Friday.

Why is his birth now commemorated on Feb 22?

Apply the corrective days used in 1752.

Show that the NS date Feb 22, 1732 fell on a Friday (use Formula II), and try to show by using Formula I that the OS date, 1731, Feb 11, fell on that *same* Friday.

Example 8. Queen Elizabeth died 1602, March 24 (old record); on what day of the week?

This is an OS uncorrected date; it was 1603, Mar 24 (Jan 1st year).

$$D_W = (5 + 3 + 0) + 3 + 3 + 5 \quad \textit{Ans. } 5\text{, Thursday.}$$

Example 9. On what day of the week will the twenty-third century begin?

This will be AD 2200, Jan 1, a *common* year. (*Section 4.*)

$$D_W = (5 + 5 + 0 + 0) + 0 + 1 + 7 \quad \textit{Ans. } 4\text{, Wednesday.}$$

Prove your answer by means of the adjustable yearly calendar.
When will Easter occur in this year? *Ans.* Apr 6.

Section 33

The Conversion Constants P, Q, R, S.

THE FUNCTION of a conversion constant is to convert an excess over a multiple of seven into the corresponding day of the week (D_W). Thus, if the excess of a given date has been found to be 3, it does not follow that D_W will be a Tuesday; it may be (3 + 6) or 2, a Monday, or some other day of the week.

In *Section 3* and *Section 32*, it was assumed that P, Q, R, S, are constants throughout the whole range of their application; that P and Q depend for their values solely on the initial conditions at the beginning of the Christian Era; that R and S depend for their values, not only on the initial conditions, but also on the modifications of the solar calendar introduced in 1582. These assumptions are now to be verified.

The common year contains $(52 \times 7 + 1)$ days and the leap year contains $(52 \times 7 + 2)$ days. The result is that in successive years, for a date preceding Feb 29, D_W will increase by one annually, but by two *after* a leap year; whereas for a date following Feb 29, D_W will increase by one annually, but by two *before* a leap year.

On the other hand, in the second member of the formula for D_W in *Section 32*, the Y-term increases by one annually, the $\frac{Y}{4}$-term increases by one every four years, and for a date after Feb 29, E_M is augmented by one in a leap year.

The interplay of these variations determines the relation of P and Q; also of R and S.

In this somewhat elusive matter it will be helpful to fix one's attention on the accompanying Table that contains the formula for D_W applied to Jan 1 of the first six years of our Era.

In AD 0, a leap year, D_W is found to be 5, or Thursday, independently of all conversion constants, by means of the adjustable civil calendar; it is clear that the constant in this year must be four to preserve the equality between the two members of the equation.

Therefore, $$P = 4$$

and P depends for its value on the initial condition that AD 0 began on Thursday.

In AD 1, D_W *after* a leap year increases by two, the Y-term increases by one; all the other terms remaining the same, the constant must be augmented by one.

Therefore, $$Q = P + 1 = 5$$

In AD 2, D_W increases by one, corresponding to the increase of one in the Y-term; the constant remains unchanged at 5.

The same obtains in AD 3.

But in AD 4, a leap year, D_W increases by one; the terms Y and $\frac{Y}{4}$ increase by one each making two in all; the other terms remaining the same, the constant 5 must be diminished by one, thus restoring 4 for a leap year, as in AD 0.

	$D_W = 6H + Y + \frac{Y}{4} + E_M + E_D +$ Constant
Jan 1, AD 0	$5 = (0 + 0 + 0) + 0 + 1 + 4$
AD 1	7 or $0 = (0 + 1 + 0) + 0 + 1 + 5$
AD 2	$1 = (0 + 2 + 0) + 0 + 1 + 5$
AD 3	$2 = (0 + 3 + 0) + 0 + 1 + 5$
AD 4	$3 = (0 + 4 + 1) + 0 + 1 + 4$
AD 5	$5 = (0 + 5 + 1) + 0 + 1 + 5$
etc.	

This interplay of changes is repeated throughout the whole Old Style calendar. P and Q are therefore true constants, connected by the relation $Q = P + 1$, and both depend for their values solely on the initial condition that Jan 1, AD 0, was a Thursday.

Now let us see what happened in 1582. The first line in the following Table gives the terms of the Old Style formula for Thursday, Oct 4, 1582.

The next day, the first of the reformed solar calendar, D_W increased by one, for the sequence of the days of the week was not disturbed; in the second member of the formula, 6H was replaced by $5H + \frac{H}{4}$, that is, 6 was replaced by (5 + 3) or 8; E_D was augmented from four to five, and by the addition of ten days, from five to fifteen. The constant must therefore be diminished by twelve, or rejecting seven, by five.

The next line in the Table shows the resulting terms, for Friday, October 15, 1582.

The OS common year constant 5 is replaced by the NS common year constant 7, or 0.

Hence, $$S = Q + 2 = 7.$$

S, therefore, depends on the initial condition at the beginning of the Era, as modified by the reform in 1582.

In 1583 the Y-term increases by one, corresponding to the increase of one in D_W; the other terms remaining the same, the constant remains at 7.

In 1584, a leap year, D_W is augmented by two; the terms Y, $\frac{Y}{4}$ and E_M are each augmented by one, and therefore the constant must be diminished by one.

Hence, $$R = S - 1 = 6.$$

In 1585 D_W increases by one; Y increases by one, E_M decreases by one, and therefore the constant must be augmented by one, thus restoring the 7 as the common year constant.

	D_W	$= 6H$		$+ Y$	$+ \frac{Y}{4}$	$+ E_M$	$+ E_D$	+ Constant
Oct 4, 1582	5	= (6		+ 5	+ 6)	+ 0	+ 4	+ 5
The Reform	+1	5H	$+ \frac{H}{4}$				+ 1 + 10	− 5
Oct 15, 1582	6	= (5	+ 3	+ 5	+ 6)	+ 0	+ 1	+ 0 or 7
Oct 15, 1583	7 or 0	= (5	+ 3	+ 6	+ 6)	+ 0	+ 1	+ 7
Oct 15, 1584	2	= (5	+ 3	+ 7	+ 7)	+ 1	+ 1	+ 6
Oct 15, 1585	3	= (5	+ 3	+ 8	+ 7)	+ 0	+ 1	+ 7
etc.								

This interplay of varying quantities continues throughout the whole range of the New Style calendar.

To sum up:

1° P, Q, R, S, are true constants throughout the whole range of their application; P and Q for use in OS dates, R and S for use in NS dates.

2° P and Q depend solely on the initial condition at the beginning of the Era, namely, on the fact that AD 0 began on a Thursday.

3° R and S depend on the initial condition as modified by the reform of 1582.

4° P, Q, R, S, are interconnected by the relations:

$$\begin{aligned} Q &= P + 1 \\ R &= Q + 1 \\ S &= R + 1 \end{aligned}$$

A *single* known date therefore suffices to determine all four constants. For example: this was written on Thursday August 24, 1939.

We have by formula: $5 = (4 + 4 + 4 + 2) + 2 + 3 + S$

Therefore, $S = 7$

and $R = S - 1$ or 6

$Q = R - 1$ or 5

$P = Q - 1$ or 4

In *Section 3* it was stated that the formulas there given for finding the dominical numbers give correct results after the intercalary day of a leap year, and consequently may be employed for the determination of Easter in *all* years as they stand, even though they use only the common year constants Q and S. The reason can now be given.

In the OS formula Q is used instead of P or $(Q - 1)$ in leap years. In such years, therefore, Q requires the correction (-1); and since Q is a term in a subtrahend, the resulting dominical number requires the correction $(+1)$ in leap years. This corrective unit however is automatically counteracted by the diminution of the dominical number by one unit, that takes place after the intercalary day to preserve the sequence of the days of the week. Hence, the dominical number found by formula is correct for *all* dates after Feb 29 whether in leap years, or in common years.

A similar reason obtains in the NS formula, where S is used instead of R or $(S - 1)$ in leap years.

Section 34

Conclusion

Such is the luni-solar calendar of the Christian Era. Since its modification under the auspices of Pope Gregory XIII in 1582, it is known as the Gregorian Calendar, and is used in most civilized countries the world over. It is a masterpiece of mathematical ingenuity, the product of many minds.

Intricate it undoubtedly is, because of the many conditions that had to be met in its construction—intricate like the works of a cathedral tower clock, whose parade of figures and play of chimes announce the passing hours. Like the tower clock, the calendar can be simplified only at the expense of some of its functions.

The new formulas and tables resulting from this study show that progress is not excluded even within the framework of this masterpiece.

The fundamental quantities on which the calendar is based are the mean tropical year and the mean astronomical lunation. It is highly improbable that these two basic units will require any appreciable change from their presently known values before AD 4800. Till then, at least, the solar calendar in its present state will keep the calendar equinox, March 21, about in the same position relatively to the mean vernal equinox that it held in 325 when the Council of Nicaea defined Easter and settled the Easter controversy; and the lunar calendar will determine the dates of the movable feasts for any year of the Christian Era—past, present, or future—in an admirably simple manner.

Should however, some interplanetary catastrophe notably alter the basic units mentioned above, it would wreck the delicate machinery of the Christian Calendar in its present form.

Summary

Practical Formulas and Methods

To find:		SECTION
Golden numbers.	Use: GN = R + 1; R from year's number ÷ 19.	2
Dominical letters.	Use: $DN = 10 - \left(6H + Y + \frac{Y}{4}\right)$ for OS years.	3
	$DN = 8 - \left(5H + \frac{H}{4} + Y + \frac{Y}{4}\right)$ for NS years.	3
	(Add one for Jan–Feb dates in leap years.)	
	Or use: (R + T) in Table I; R from year's number ÷ 28.	3
Annual epacts.	Use: GN with Table IV.	9
Mart. letters.	Use: GN with Table XIX.	29
	Or use: annual epact with Table in Section 14.	14
Movable feasts.	Use: GN and DL with Table XVIII.	28
	Or use: annual epact and DL with Tables X or XI. (For NS years only.)	15
	Or use: GN and DL with Table XIV. (For OS years only.)	16
Day of week.	Use: the adjustable calendar with DL as setting	31
	Or use: DL with Table IX.	3
	Or use:	
	$D_W = \left(6H + Y + \frac{Y}{4}\right) + E_M + E_D + \begin{cases} 4 \text{ in OS leap yrs.} \\ 5 \text{ in OS common yrs.} \end{cases}$	
	$D_W = \left(5H + \frac{H}{4} + Y + \frac{Y}{4}\right) + E_M + E_D + \begin{cases} 6 \text{ in NS leap yrs.} \\ 7 \text{ in NS common yrs.} \end{cases}$	
	where $E_M = 3(M - 2) - N_{30} + 1_L$.	32

TABLES

TABLE I

To find Dominical Letters

Periods	T
AD 0–1582	0
1582–1700	20
1701–1800	8
1801–1900	24
1901–2100	12
2101–2200	0
2201–2300	16
2301–2500	4
2501–2600	20
2601–2700	8
2701–2900	24
2901–3000	12
3001–3100	0
3101–3300	16
3301–3400	4
3401–3500	20
3501–3700	8
3701–3800	24
3801–3900	12
3901–4100	0
4101–4200	16
4201–4300	4
4301–4500	20
4501–4600	8
4601–4700	24
4701–4900	12
4901–5000	0
etc.	etc.

R + T	DL
0	DC
1	B
2	A
3	G
4	FE
5	D
6	C
7	B
8	AG
9	F
10	E
11	D
12	CB
13	A
14	G
15	F
16	ED
17	C
18	B
19	A
20	GF
21	E
22	D
23	C
24	BA
25	G
26	F
27	E

Find R from year's number ÷ 28; T from Table.
Explanation in *Section 3*.

TABLE II

The Gregorian 400-year Solar Cycle

		49	−.12	101	+.49	153	+.10	205	+.71	257	+.32	309	+.93	361	+.54
		50	+.13	102	+.74	154	+.35	206	+.96	258	+.57	310	+1.18	362	+.79
		51	+.37	103	+.98	155	+.59	207	+1.20	259	+.81	311	+1.42	363	+1.03
Year	Corr.	52	−.39	104	+.22	156	−.17	208	+.44	260	+.05	312	+.66	364	+.27
1	+.24	53	−.15	105	+.46	157	+.07	209	+.68	261	+.29	313	+.90	365	+.51
2	+.49	54	+.10	106	+.71	158	+.32	210	+.93	262	+.54	314	+1.15	366	+.76
3	+.73	55	+.34	107	+.95	159	+.56	211	+1.17	263	+.78	315	+1.39	367	+1.00
4	−.03	56	−.42	108	+.19	160	−.20	212	+.41	264	+.02	316	+.63	368	+.24
5	+.21	57	−.18	109	+.43	161	+.04	213	+.65	265	+.26	317	+.87	369	+.48
6	+.46	58	+.07	110	+.68	162	+.29	214	+.90	266	+.51	318	+1.12	370	+.73
7	+.70	59	+.31	111	+.92	163	+.53	215	+1.14	267	+.75	319	+1.36	371	+.97
8	−.06	60	−.45	112	+.16	164	−.23	216	+.38	268	−.01	320	+.60	372	+.21
9	+.18	61	−.21	113	+.40	165	+.01	217	+.62	269	+.23	321	+.84	373	+.45
10	+.43	62	+.04	114	+.65	166	+.26	218	+.87	270	+.48	322	+1.09	374	+.70
11	+.67	63	+.28	115	+.89	167	+.50	219	+1.11	271	+.72	323	+1.33	375	+.94
12	−.09	64	−.48	116	+.13	168	−.26	220	+.35	272	−.04	324	+.57	376	+.18
13	+.15	65	−.24	117	+.37	169	−.02	221	+.59	273	+.20	325	+.81	377	+.42
14	+.40	66	+.01	118	+.62	170	+.23	222	+.84	274	+.45	326	+1.06	378	+.67
15	+.64	67	+.25	119	+.86	171	+.47	223	+1.08	275	+.69	327	+1.30	379	+.91
16	−.12	68	−.51	120	+.10	172	−.29	224	+.32	276	−.07	328	+.54	380	+.15
17	+.12	69	−.27	121	+.34	173	−.05	225	+.56	277	+.17	329	+.78	381	+.39
18	+.37	70	−.03	122	+.59	174	+.20	226	+.81	278	+.42	330	+1.03	382	+.64
19	+.61	71	+.22	123	+.83	175	+.44	227	+1.05	279	+.66	331	+1.27	383	+.88
20	−.15	72	−.54	124	+.07	176	−.32	228	+.29	280	−.10	332	+.51	384	+.12
21	+.09	73	−.30	125	+.31	177	−.08	229	+.53	281	+.14	333	+.75	385	+.36
22	+.34	74	−.06	126	+.56	178	+.17	230	+.78	282	+.39	334	+1.00	386	+.61
23	+.58	75	+.19	127	+.80	179	+.41	231	+1.02	283	+.63	335	+1.24	387	+.85
24	−.18	76	−.57	128	+.04	180	−.35	232	+.26	284	−.13	336	+.48	388	+.09

25	+.06	77	−.33	129	+.29	181	−.11	233	+.50	285	+.11	337	+.72	389	+.33
26	+.31	78	−.09	130	+.53	182	+.14	234	+.75	286	+.36	338	+.97	390	+.58
27	+.55	79	+.16	131	+.77	183	+.38	235	+.99	287	+.60	339	+1.21	391	+.82
28	−.22	80	−.60	132	+.01	184	−.38	236	+.23	288	−.16	340	+.45	392	+.06
29	+.03	81	−.36	133	+.25	185	−.14	237	+.47	289	+.08	341	+.69	393	+.30
30	+.28	82	−.12	134	+.50	186	+.11	238	+.72	290	+.33	342	+.94	394	+.55
31	+.52	83	+.13	135	+.74	187	+.35	239	+.96	291	+.57	343	+1.18	395	+.79
32	−.24	84	−.63	136	−.02	188	−.41	240	+.20	292	−.19	344	+.42	396	+.03
33	+.01	85	−.39	137	+.22	189	−.17	241	+.44	293	+.05	345	+.66	397	+.27
34	+.25	86	−.15	138	+.47	190	+.08	242	+.69	294	+.30	346	+.91	398	+.52
35	+.49	87	+.10	139	+.71	191	+.32	243	+.93	295	+.54	347	+1.15	399	+.76
36	−.27	88	−.66	140	−.05	192	−.44	244	+.17	296	−.22	348	+.39	400	0.00
37	−.03	89	−.42	141	+.19	193	−.20	245	+.41	297	+.02	349	+.63	1	+.24
38	+.22	90	−.18	142	+.44	194	+.05	246	+.66	298	+.27	350	+.88	2	+.49
39	+.46	91	+.07	143	+.68	195	+.29	247	+.90	299	+.51	351	+1.12	3	+.73
40	−.30	92	−.69	144	−.08	196	−.47	248	+.14	300	+.75	352	+.36	etc.	
41	−.06	93	−.45	145	+.16	197	−.23	249	+.38	301	+.99	353	+.60		
42	+.19	94	−.21	146	+.41	198	+.02	250	+.63	302	+1.24	354	+.85		
43	+.43	95	+.04	147	+.65	199	+.26	251	+.87	303 M	+1.48	355	+1.09		
44	−.33	96 m	−.72	148	−.11	200	+.50	252	+.11	304	+.72	356	+.33		
45	−.09	97	−.48	149	+.13	201	+.74	253	+.35	305	+.96	357	+.57		
46	+.16	98	−.24	150	+.38	202	+.99	254	+.60	306	+1.21	358	+.82		
47	+.40	99	+.01	151	+.62	203	+1.23	255	+.84	307	+1.45	359	+1.06		
48	−.36	100	+.25	152	−.14	204	+.47	256	+.08	308	+.69	360	+.30		

Explanation in *Section 5.*

TABLE III

Lunar and Solar Equations Applied to Epacts

Year	Lun Equ	Sol Equ	Epact Series	Year	Lun Equ	Sol Equ	Epact Series	Year	Lun Equ	Sol Equ	Epact Series
AD 0			VIII etc.								
100		—1	VII	3700		—1	XXII	7300		—1	VI
200	+1	—1		3800		—1	XXI	7400	+1	—1	
300		—1	VI	3900	+1	—1		7500		—1	V
400				4000				7600			
500	+1	—1		4100		—1	XX	7700	+1	—1	
600		—1	V	4200		—1	XIX	7800		—1	IV
700		—1	IV	4300	+1	—1		7900		—1	III
800	+1		V	4400				8000	+1		IV
900		—1	IV	4500		—1	XVIII	8100		—1	III
1000		—1	III	4600	+1	—1		8200		—1	II
1100	+1	—1		4700		—1	XVII	8300	+1	—1	
1200				4800				8400			
1300		—1	II	4900	+1	—1		8500		—1	I
1400	+1	—1		5000		—1	XVI	8600	+1	—1	
1500		—1	I	5100		—1	XV	8700		—1	*
1600				5200	+1		XVI	8800			
1700		—1	*	5300		—1	XV	8900	+1	—1	
1800	+1	—1		5400		—1	XIV	9000		—1	XXIX
1900		—1	XXIX	5500	+1	—1		9100		—1	XXVIII
2000				5600				9200			
2100	+1	—1		5700		—1	XIII	9300	+1	—1	
2200		—1	XXVIII	5800	+1	—1		9400		—1	XXVII
2300		—1	XXVII	5900		—1	XII	9500		—1	XXVI
2400	+1		XXVIII	6000				9600	+1		XXVII
2500		—1	XXVII	6100	+1	—1		9700		—1	XXVI
2600		—1	XXVI	6200		—1	XI	9800		—1	XXV
2700	+1	—1		6300		—1	X	9900	+1	—1	
2800				6400	+1		XI	10000			
2900		—1	XXV	6500		—1	X	10100		—1	XXIV
3000	+1	—1		6600		—1	IX	10200	+1	—1	
3100		—1	XXIV	6700		—1	VIII	10300		—1	XXIII
3200				6800	+1		IX	10400			
3300	+1	—1		6900		—1	VIII	10500	+1	—1	
3400		—1	XXIII	7000		—1	VII	10600		—1	XXII
3500		—1	XXII	7100	+1	—1		10700		—1	XXI
3600	+1		XXIII	7200				10800	+1		XXII

Explanation in *Section 9* and *Section 10.*

TABLE IV

Various Series of Reformed Epacts and Their Periods

GN =	1	2	3	4	5	6	7	8	9	10	11	12	13	14	15	16	17	18	19
Year	Epacts																		
AD 0	8	19	*	11	22	3	14	25	6	17	28	9	20	1	12	23	4	15	26
1582	1	12	23	4	15	26	7	18	29	10	21	2	13	24	5	16	27	8	[19]
1700	*	11	22	3	14	25	6	17	28	9	20	1	12	23	4	15	26	7	18
1900	29	10	21	2	13	24	5	16	27	8	19	*	11	22	3	14	[25]	6	17
2200	28	9	20	1	12	23	4	15	26	7	18	29	10	21	2	13	24	5	16
2300	27	8	19	*	11	22	3	14	25	6	17	28	9	20	1	12	23	4	15
2400	28	9	20	1	12	23	4	15	26	7	18	29	10	21	2	13	24	5	16
2500	27	8	19	*	11	22	3	14	25	6	17	28	9	20	1	12	23	4	15
2600	26	7	18	29	10	21	2	13	24	5	16	27	8	19	*	11	22	3	14
2900	25	6	17	28	9	20	1	12	23	4	15	26	7	18	29	10	21	2	13
3100	24	5	16	27	8	19	*	11	22	3	14	[25]	6	17	28	9	20	1	12
3400	23	4	15	26	7	18	29	10	21	2	13	24	5	16	27	8	19	*	11
3500	22	3	14	25	6	17	28	9	20	1	12	23	4	15	26	7	18	29	10
3600	23	4	15	26	7	18	29	10	21	2	13	24	5	16	27	8	19	*	11
3700	22	3	14	25	6	17	28	9	20	1	12	23	4	15	26	7	18	29	10
3800	21	2	13	24	5	16	27	8	19	*	11	22	3	14	[25]	6	17	28	9
4100	20	1	12	23	4	15	26	7	18	29	10	21	2	13	24	5	16	27	8
etc.																			

Explanation in *Section 9.*

TABLE V

New Style 19-year Cycle of New Moon Dates

(Used from 1582 to 1699)

GN	Epacts													
1	I	Jan 30 29	Feb 28 30	Mar 30 29	Apr 28 30	May 28 29	Jun 26 30	Jul 26 29	Aug 24 30	Sep 23 29	Oct 22 30	Nov 21 29	Dec 20 30	
2	XII	Jan 19 29	Feb 17 30	Mar 19 29	Apr 17 30	May 17 29	Jun 15 30	Jul 15 29	Aug 13 30	Sep 12 29	Oct 11 30	Nov 10 29	Dec 9 30	
3	XXIII	Jan 8 29	Feb 6 30	Mar 8 29	Apr 6 30	May 6 29	Jun 4 30	Jul 4 29	Aug 2 30	Sep 1 29	Sep 30 30	Oct 30 29	Nov 28 30	Dec 28 □
4	IV	Jan 27 29	Feb 25 30	Mar 27 29	Apr 25 30	May 25 29	Jun 23 30	Jul 23 29	Aug 21 30	Sep 20 29	Oct 19 30	Nov 18 29	Dec 17 30	
5	XV	Jan 16 29	Feb 14 30	Mar 16 29	Apr 14 30	May 14 29	Jun 12 30	Jul 12 29	Aug 10 30	Sep 9 29	Oct 8 30	Nov 7 29	Dec 6 30	
6	XXVI	Jan 5 □	Feb 4 29	Mar 5 30	Apr 4 29	May 3 30	Jun 2 29	Jul 1 30	Jul 31 29	Aug 29 30	Sep 28 29	Oct 27 30	Nov 26 29	Dec 25 30
7	VII	Jan 24 29	Feb 22 30	Mar 24 29	Apr 22 30	May 22 29	Jun 20 30	Jul 20 29	Aug 18 30	Sep 17 29	Oct 16 30	Nov 15 29	Dec 14 30	
8	XVIII	Jan 13 29	Feb 11 30	Mar 13 29	Apr 11 30	May 11 29	Jun 9 30	Jul 9 29	Aug 7 30	Sep 6 29	Oct 5 30	Nov 4 29	Dec 3 30	
9	XXIX	Jan 2 □	Feb 1 29	Mar 2 30	Apr 1 29	Apr 30 30	May 30 29	Jun 28 30	Jul 28 29	Aug 26 30	Sep 25 29	Oct 24 30	Nov 23 29	Dec 22 30
10	X	Jan 21 29	Feb 19 30	Mar 21 29	Apr 19 30	May 19 29	Jun 17 30	Jul 17 29	Aug 15 30	Sep 14 29	Oct 13 30	Nov 12 29	Dec 11 30	
11	XXI	Jan 10 29	Feb 8 30	Mar 10 29	Apr 8 30	May 8 29	Jun 6 30	Jul 6 29	Aug 4 30	Sep 3 29	Oct 2 30	Nov 1 29	Nov 30 30	Dec 30 □
12	II	Jan 29 29	Feb 27 30	Mar 29 29	Apr 27 30	May 27 29	Jun 25 30	Jul 25 29	Aug 23 30	Sep 22 29	Oct 21 30	Nov 20 29	Dec 19 30	
13	XIII	Jan 18 29	Feb 16 30	Mar 18 29	Apr 16 30	May 16 29	Jun 14 30	Jul 14 29	Aug 12 30	Sep 11 29	Oct 10 30	Nov 9 29	Dec 8 30	

14	XXIV	Jan 7 29	Feb 5 30	Mar 7 29	Apr 5 30	May 5 29	Jun 3 30	Jul 3 29	Aug 1 30	Aug 31 29	Sep 29 30	Oct 29 29	Nov 27 30	Dec 27 □
15	V	Jan 26 29	Feb 24 30	Mar 26 29	Apr 24 30	May 24 29	Jun 22 30	Jul 22 29	Aug 20 30	Sep 19 29	Oct 18 30	Nov 17 29	Dec 16 30	
16	XVI	Jan 15 29	Feb 13 30	Mar 15 29	Apr 13 30	May 13 29	Jun 11 30	Jul 11 29	Aug 9 30	Sep 8 29	Oct 7 30	Nov 6 29	Dec 5 30	
17	XXVII	Jan 4 □	Feb 3 29	Mar 4 30	Apr 3 29	May 2 30	Jun 1 29	Jun 30 30	Jul 30 29	Aug 28 30	Sep 27 29	Oct 26 30	Nov 25 29	Dec 24 30
18	VIII	Jan 23 29	Feb 21 30	Mar 23 29	Apr 21 30	May 21 29	Jun 19 30	Jul 19 29	Aug 17 30	Sep 16 29	Oct 15 30	Nov 14 29	Dec 13 30	
19	XIX	Jan 12 29	Feb 10 30	Mar 12 29	Apr 10 30	May 10 29	Jun 8 30	Jul 8 29	Aug 6 30	Sep 5 29	Oct 4 30	Nov 3 29	Dec 2 □−1	Dec 31 30
	+XII													
1	I	Jan 30 etc.												

The symbol □ means $(29\frac{1}{2} + \frac{1}{2})$ or 30 days.
Explanation in *Section 8*.

TABLE VI

New Style 19-year Cycle of New Moon Dates

(Used from 1900 to 2199)

GN	Epact													
1	XXIX	Jan 2 □	Feb 1 29	Mar 2 30	Apr 1 29	Apr 30 30	May 30 29	Jun 28 30	Jul 28 29	Aug 26 30	Sep 25 29	Oct 24 30	Nov 23 29	Dec 22 30
2	X	Jan 21 29	Feb 19 30	Mar 21 29	Apr 19 30	May 19 29	Jun 17 30	Jul 17 29	Aug 15 30	Sep 14 29	Oct 13 30	Nov 12 29	Dec 11 30	
3	XXI	Jan 10 29	Feb 8 30	Mar 10 29	Apr 8 30	May 8 29	Jun 6 30	Jul 6 29	Aug 4 30	Sep 3 29	Oct 2 30	Nov 1 29	Nov 30 30	Dec 30 □
4	II	Jan 29 29	Feb 27 30	Mar 29 29	Apr 27 30	May 27 29	Jun 25 30	Jul 25 29	Aug 23 30	Sep 22 29	Oct 21 30	Nov 20 29	Dec 19 30	
5	XIII	Jan 18 29	Feb 16 30	Mar 18 29	Apr 16 30	May 16 29	Jun 14 30	Jul 14 29	Aug 12 30	Sep 11 29	Oct 10 30	Nov 9 29	Dec 8 30	
6	XXIV	Jan 7 29	Feb 5 30	Mar 7 29	Apr 5 30	May 5 29	Jun 3 30	Jul 3 29	Aug 1 30	Aug 31 29	Sep 29 30	Oct 29 29	Nov 27 30	Dec 27 □
7	V	Jan 26 29	Feb 24 30	Mar 26 29	Apr 24 30	May 24 29	Jun 22 30	Jul 22 29	Aug 20 30	Sep 19 29	Oct 18 30	Nov 17 29	Dec 16 30	
8	XVI	Jan 15 29	Feb 13 30	Mar 15 29	Apr 13 30	May 13 29	Jun 11 30	Jul 11 29	Aug 9 30	Sep 8 29	Oct 7 30	Nov 6 29	Dec 5 30	
9	XXVII	Jan 4 □	Feb 3 29	Mar 4 30	Apr 3 29	May 2 30	Jun 1 29	Jun 30 30	Jul 30 29	Aug 28 30	Sep 27 29	Oct 26 30	Nov 25 29	Dec 24 30
10	VIII	Jan 23 29	Feb 21 30	Mar 23 29	Apr 21 30	May 21 29	Jun 19 30	Jul 19 29	Aug 17 30	Sep 16 29	Oct 15 30	Nov 14 29	Dec 13 30	
11	XIX	Jan 12 29	Feb 10 30	Mar 12 29	Apr 10 30	May 10 29	Jun 8 30	Jul 8 29	Aug 6 30	Sep 5 29	Oct 4 30	Nov 3 29	Dec 2 30	
12	*	Jan 1 □	Jan 31 29	Mar 1 30	Mar 31 29	Apr 29 30	May 29 29	Jun 27 30	Jul 27 29	Aug 25 30	Sep 24 29	Oct 23 30	Nov 22 29	Dec 21 30
13	XI	Jan 20 29	Feb 18 30	Mar 20 29	Apr 18 30	May 18 29	Jun 16 30	Jul 16 29	Aug 14 30	Sep 13 29	Oct 12 30	Nov 11 29	Dec 10 30	

14	XXII	Jan 9 29	Feb 7 30	Mar 9 29	Apr 7 30	May 7 29	Jun 5 30	Jul 5 29	Aug 3 30	Sep 2 29	Oct 1 30	Oct 31 29	Nov 29 30	Dec 29 □
15	III	Jan 28 29	Feb 26 30	Mar 28 29	Apr 26 30	May 26 29	Jun 24 30	Jul 24 29	Aug 22 30	Sep 21 29	Oct 20 30	Nov 19 29	Dec 18 30	
16	XIV	Jan 17 29	Feb 15 30	Mar 17 29	Apr 15 30	May 15 29	Jun 13 30	Jul 13 29	Aug 11 30	Sep 10 29	Oct 9 30	Nov 8 29	Dec 7 30	
17	[25]	Jan 6 29	Feb 4 30	Mar 6 29	Apr 4 30	May 4 29	Jun 2 30	Jul 2 29	Jul 31 30	Aug 30 29	Sep 28 30	Oct 28 29	Nov 26 30	Dec 26 □
18	VI	Jan 25 29	Feb 23 30	Mar 25 29	Apr 23 30	May 23 29	Jun 21 30	Jul 21 29	Aug 19 30	Sep 18 29	Oct 17 30	Nov 16 29	Dec 15 30	
19	XVII	Jan 14 29	Feb 12 30	Mar 14 29	Apr 12 30	May 12 29	Jun 10 30	Jul 10 29	Aug 8 30	Sep 7 29	Oct 6 30	Nov 5 29	Dec 4 30–1	
	+XII													
1	XXIX	Jan 2 etc.												

The symbol □ means ($29\frac{1}{2} + \frac{1}{2}$) or 30 days.
Explanation in *Section 8*.

TABLE VII

Thirty-year Cycle of New Moon Dates

Epact													
*	Jan 1 □	Jan 31 29	Mar 1 30	Mar 31 29	Apr 29 30	May 29 29	Jun 27 30	Jul 27 29	Aug 25 30	Sep 24 29	Oct 23 30	Nov 22 29	Dec 21 30
XI	Jan 20 29	Feb 18 30	Mar 20 29	Apr 18 30	May 18 29	Jun 16 30	Jul 16 29	Aug 14 30	Sep 13 29	Oct 12 30	Nov 11 29	Dec 10 30	
XXII	Jan 9 29	Feb 7 30	Mar 9 29	Apr 7 30	May 7 29	Jun 5 30	Jul 5 29	Aug 3 30	Sep 2 29	Oct 1 30	Oct 31 29	Nov 29 30	Dec 29 □
III	Jan 28 29	Feb 26 30	Mar 28 29	Apr 26 30	May 26 29	Jun 24 30	Jul 24 29	Aug 22 30	Sep 21 29	Oct 20 30	Nov 19 29	Dec 18 30	
XIV	Jan 17 29	Feb 15 30	Mar 17 29	Apr 15 30	May 15 29	Jun 13 30	Jul 13 29	Aug 11 30	Sep 10 29	Oct 9 30	Nov 8 29	Dec 7 30	
XXV	Jan 6 □	Feb 5 29	Mar 6 30	Apr 5 29	May 4 30	Jun 3 29	Jul 2 30	Aug 1 29	Aug 30 30	Sep 29 29	Oct 28 30	Nov 27 29	Dec 26 30
VI	Jan 25 29	Feb 23 30	Mar 25 29	Apr 23 30	May 23 29	Jun 21 30	Jul 21 29	Aug 19 30	Sep 18 29	Oct 17 30	Nov 16 29	Dec 15 30	
XVII	Jan 14 29	Feb 12 30	Mar 14 29	Apr 12 30	May 12 29	Jun 10 30	Jul 10 29	Aug 8 30	Sep 7 29	Oct 6 30	Nov 5 29	Dec 4 30	
XXVIII	Jan 3 □	Feb 2 29	Mar 3 30	Apr 2 29	May 1 30	May 31 29	Jun 29 30	Jul 29 29	Aug 27 30	Sep 26 29	Oct 25 30	Nov 24 29	Dec 23 30
IX	Jan 22 29	Feb 20 30	Mar 22 29	Apr 20 30	May 20 29	Jun 18 30	Jul 18 29	Aug 16 30	Sep 15 29	Oct 14 30	Nov 13 29	Dec 12 30	
XX	Jan 11 29	Feb 9 30	Mar 11 29	Apr 9 30	May 9 29	Jun 7 30	Jul 7 29	Aug 5 30	Sep 4 29	Oct 3 30	Nov 2 29	Dec 1 30	Dec 31 □
I	Jan 30 29	Feb 28 30	Mar 30 29	Apr 28 30	May 28 29	Jun 26 30	Jul 26 29	Aug 24 30	Sep 23 29	Oct 22 30	Nov 21 29	Dec 20 30	
XII	Jan 19 29	Feb 17 30	Mar 19 29	Apr 17 30	May 17 29	Jun 15 30	Jul 15 29	Aug 13 30	Sep 12 29	Oct 11 30	Nov 10 29	Dec 9 30	
XXIII	Jan 8 29	Feb 6 30	Mar 8 29	Apr 6 30	May 6 29	Jun 4 30	Jul 4 29	Aug 2 30	Sep 1 29	Sep 30 30	Oct 30 29	Nov 28 30	Dec 28 □
IV	Jan 27 29	Feb 25 30	Mar 27 29	Apr 25 30	May 25 29	Jun 23 30	Jul 23 29	Aug 21 30	Sep 20 29	Oct 19 30	Nov 18 29	Dec 17 30	

XV	Jan 16 29	Feb 14 30	Mar 16 29	Apr 14 30	May 14 29	Jun 12 30	Jul 12 29	Aug 10 30	Sep 9 29	Oct 8 30	Nov 7 29	Dec 6 30	
XXVI	Jan 5 □	Feb 4 29	Mar 5 30	Apr 4 29	May 3 30	Jun 2 29	Jul 1 30	Jul 31 29	Aug 29 30	Sep 28 29	Oct 27 30	Nov 26 29	Dec 25 30
VII	Jan 24 29	Feb 22 30	Mar 24 29	Apr 22 30	May 22 29	Jun 20 30	Jul 20 29	Aug 18 30	Sep 17 29	Oct 16 30	Nov 15 29	Dec 14 30	
XVIII	Jan 13 29	Feb 11 30	Mar 13 29	Apr 11 30	May 11 29	Jun 9 30	Jul 9 29	Aug 7 30	Sep 6 29	Oct 5 30	Nov 4 29	Dec 3 30	
XXIX	Jan 2 □	Feb 1 29	Mar 2 30	Apr 1 29	Apr 30 30	May 30 29	Jun 28 30	Jul 28 29	Aug 26 30	Sep 25 29	Oct 24 30	Nov 23 29	Dec 22 30
X	Jan 21 29	Feb 19 30	Mar 21 29	Apr 19 30	May 19 29	Jun 17 30	Jul 17 29	Aug 15 30	Sep 14 29	Oct 13 30	Nov 12 29	Dec 11 30	
XXI	Jan 10 29	Feb 8 30	Mar 10 29	Apr 8 30	May 8 29	Jun 6 30	Jul 6 29	Aug 4 30	Sep 3 29	Oct 2 30	Nov 1 29	Nov 30 30	Dec 30 □
II	Jan 29 29	Feb 27 30	Mar 29 29	Apr 27 30	May 27 29	Jun 25 30	Jul 25 29	Aug 23 30	Sep 22 29	Oct 21 30	Nov 20 29	Dec 19 30	
XIII	Jan 18 29	Feb 16 30	Mar 18 29	Apr 16 30	May 16 29	Jun 14 30	Jul 14 29	Aug 12 30	Sep 11 29	Oct 10 30	Nov 9 29	Dec 8 30	
XXIV	Jan 7 29	Feb 5 30	Mar 7 29	Apr 5 30	May 5 29	Jun 3 30	Jul 3 29	Aug 1 30	Aug 31 29	Sep 29 30	Oct 29 29	Nov 27 30	Dec 27 □
V	Jan 26 29	Feb 24 30	Mar 26 29	Apr 24 30	May 24 29	Jun 22 30	Jul 22 29	Aug 20 30	Sep 19 29	Oct 18 30	Nov 17 29	Dec 16 30	
XVI	Jan 15 29	Feb 13 30	Mar 15 29	Apr 13 30	May 13 29	Jun 11 30	Jul 11 29	Aug 9 30	Sep 8 29	Oct 7 30	Nov 6 29	Dec 5 30	
XXVII	Jan 4 □	Feb 3 29	Mar 4 30	Apr 3 29	May 2 30	Jun 1 29	Jun 30 30	Jul 30 29	Aug 28 30	Sep 27 29	Oct 26 30	Nov 25 29	Dec 24 30
VIII	Jan 23 29	Feb 21 30	Mar 23 29	Apr 21 30	May 21 29	Jun 19 30	Jul 19 29	Aug 17 30	Sep 16 29	Oct 15 30	Nov 14 29	Dec 13 30	
XIX	Jan 12 29	Feb 10 30	Mar 12 29	Apr 10 30	May 10 29	Jun 8 30	Jul 8 29	Aug 6 30	Sep 5 29	Oct 4 30	Nov 3 29	Dec 2 30	
*	Jan 1 etc.												

The symbol □ means ($29\frac{1}{2} + \frac{1}{2}$) or 30 days.
Explanation in *Section 11*.

TABLE VIII

Re-arranged Thirty-year Cycle

Epact													
*	Jan 1 □	Jan 31 29	Mar 1 30	Mar 31 29	Apr 29 30	May 29 29	Jun 27 30	Jul 27 29	Aug 25 30	Sep 24 29	Oct 23 30	Nov 22 29	Dec 21 30
XXIX	Jan 2 □	Feb 1 29	Mar 2 30	Apr 1 29	Apr 30 30	May 30 29	Jun 28 30	Jul 28 29	Aug 26 30	Sep 25 29	Oct 24 30	Nov 23 29	Dec 22 30
XXVIII	Jan 3 □	Feb 2 29	Mar 3 30	Apr 2 29	May 1 30	May 31 29	Jun 29 30	Jul 29 29	Aug 27 30	Sep 26 29	Oct 25 30	Nov 24 29	Dec 23 30
XXVII	Jan 4 □	Feb 3 29	Mar 4 30	Apr 3 29	May 2 30	Jun 1 29	Jun 30 30	Jul 30 29	Aug 28 30	Sep 27 29	Oct 26 30	Nov 25 29	Dec 24 30
XXVI	Jan 5 □	Feb 4 29	Mar 5 30	Apr 4 29	May 3 30	Jun 2 29	Jul 1 30	Jul 31 29	Aug 29 30	Sep 28 29	Oct 27 30	Nov 26 29	Dec 25 30
XXV	Jan 6 □	(Feb 5) 29	Mar 6 30	(Apr 5) 29	May 4 30	(Jun 3) 29	Jul 2 30	(Aug 1) 29	Aug 30 30	(Sep 29) 29	Oct 28 30	(Nov 27) 29	Dec 26 30
XXIV	Jan 7 29	Feb 5 30	Mar 7 29	Apr 5 30	May 5 29	Jun 3 30	Jul 3 29	Aug 1 30	Aug 31 29	Sep 29 30	Oct 29 29	Nov 27 30	Dec 27 □
XXIII	Jan 8 29	Feb 6 30	Mar 8 29	Apr 6 30	May 6 29	Jun 4 30	Jul 4 29	Aug 2 30	Sep 1 29	Sep 30 30	Oct 30 29	Nov 28 30	Dec 28 □
XXII	Jan 9 29	Feb 7 30	Mar 9 29	Apr 7 30	May 7 29	Jun 5 30	Jul 5 29	Aug 3 30	Sep 2 29	Oct 1 30	Oct 31 29	Nov 29 30	Dec 29 □
XXI	Jan 10 29	Feb 8 30	Mar 10 29	Apr 8 30	May 8 29	Jun 6 30	Jul 6 29	Aug 4 30	Sep 3 29	Oct 2 30	Nov 1 29	Nov 30 30	Dec 30 □
XX	Jan 11 29	Feb 9 30	Mar 11 29	Apr 9 30	May 9 29	Jun 7 30	Jul 7 29	Aug 5 30	Sep 4 29	Oct 3 30	Nov 2 29	Dec 1 30	Dec 31 □
XIX	Jan 12 29	Feb 10 30	Mar 12 29	Apr 10 30	May 10 29	Jun 8 30	Jul 8 29	Aug 6 30	Sep 5 29	Oct 4 30	Nov 3 29	Dec 2 30	
XVIII	Jan 13 29	Feb 11 30	Mar 13 29	Apr 11 30	May 11 29	Jun 9 30	Jul 9 29	Aug 7 30	Sep 6 29	Oct 5 30	Nov 4 29	Dec 3 30	
XVII	Jan 14 29	Feb 12 30	Mar 14 29	Apr 12 30	May 12 29	Jun 10 30	Jul 10 29	Aug 8 30	Sep 7 29	Oct 6 30	Nov 5 29	Dec 4 30	
XVI	Jan 15 29	Feb 13 30	Mar 15 29	Apr 13 30	May 13 29	Jun 11 30	Jul 11 29	Aug 9 30	Sep 8 29	Oct 7 30	Nov 6 29	Dec 5 30	

XV	Jan 16 29	Feb 14 30	Mar 16 29	Apr 14 30	May 14 29	Jun 12 30	Jul 12 29	Aug 10 30	Sep 9 29	Oct 8 30	Nov 7 29	Dec 6 30
XIV	Jan 17 29	Feb 15 30	Mar 17 29	Apr 15 30	May 15 29	Jun 13 30	Jul 13 29	Aug 11 30	Sep 10 29	Oct 9 30	Nov 8 29	Dec 7 30
XIII	Jan 18 29	Feb 16 30	Mar 18 29	Apr 16 30	May 16 29	Jun 14 30	Jul 14 29	Aug 12 30	Sep 11 29	Oct 10 30	Nov 9 29	Dec 8 30
XII	Jan 19 29	Feb 17 30	Mar 19 29	Apr 17 30	May 17 29	Jun 15 30	Jul 15 29	Aug 13 30	Sep 12 29	Oct 11 30	Nov 10 29	Dec 9 30
XI	Jan 20 29	Feb 18 30	Mar 20 29	Apr 18 30	May 18 29	Jun 16 30	Jul 16 29	Aug 14 30	Sep 13 29	Oct 12 30	Nov 11 29	Dec 10 30
X	Jan 21 29	Feb 19 30	Mar 21 29	Apr 19 30	May 19 29	Jun 17 30	Jul 17 29	Aug 15 30	Sep 14 29	Oct 13 30	Nov 12 29	Dec 11 30
IX	Jan 22 29	Feb 20 30	Mar 22 29	Apr 20 30	May 20 29	Jun 18 30	Jul 18 29	Aug 16 30	Sep 15 29	Oct 14 30	Nov 13 29	Dec 12 30
VIII	Jan 23 29	Feb 21 30	Mar 23 29	Apr 21 30	May 21 29	Jun 19 30	Jul 19 29	Aug 17 30	Sep 16 29	Oct 15 30	Nov 14 29	Dec 13 30
VII	Jan 24 29	Feb 22 30	Mar 24 29	Apr 22 30	May 22 29	Jun 20 30	Jul 20 29	Aug 18 30	Sep 17 29	Oct 16 30	Nov 15 29	Dec 14 30
VI	Jan 25 29	Feb 23 30	Mar 25 29	Apr 23 30	May 23 29	Jun 21 30	Jul 21 29	Aug 19 30	Sep 18 29	Oct 17 30	Nov 16 29	Dec 15 30
V	Jan 26 29	Feb 24 30	Mar 26 29	Apr 24 30	May 24 29	Jun 22 30	Jul 22 29	Aug 20 30	Sep 19 29	Oct 18 30	Nov 17 29	Dec 16 30
IV	Jan 27 29	Feb 25 30	Mar 27 29	Apr 25 30	May 25 29	Jun 23 30	Jul 23 29	Aug 21 30	Sep 20 29	Oct 19 30	Nov 18 29	Dec 17 30
III	Jan 28 29	Feb 26 30	Mar 28 29	Apr 26 30	May 26 29	Jun 24 30	Jul 24 29	Aug 22 30	Sep 21 29	Oct 20 30	Nov 19 29	Dec 18 30
II	Jan 29 29	Feb 27 30	Mar 29 29	Apr 27 30	May 27 29	Jun 25 30	Jul 25 29	Aug 23 30	Sep 22 29	Oct 21 30	Nov 20 29	Dec 19 30
I	Jan 30 29	Feb 28 30	Mar 30 29	Apr 28 30	May 28 29	Jun 26 30	Jul 26 29	Aug 24 30	Sep 23 29	Oct 22 30	Nov 21 29	Dec 20 30

The symbol □ means ($29\frac{1}{2} + \frac{1}{2}$) or 30 days.
Explanation in *Section 11*.

TABLE IX

New Style Yearly Calendar

(Used since 1582)

January Epact DL	February	March	April	May	June
* A 1	XXIX D 1	* D 1	XXIX G 1	XXVIII B 1	XXVII E 1
XXIX B 2	XXVIII E 2	XXIX E 2	XXVIII A 2	XXVII C 2	[25] XXVI F 2
XXVIII C 3	XXVII F 3	XXVIII F 3	XXVII B 3	XXVI D 3	XXV, XXIV G 3
XXVII D 4	[25] XXVI G 4	XXVII G 4	[25] XXVI C 4	[25] XXV E 4	XXIII A 4
XXVI E 5	XXV, XXIV A 5	XXVI A 5	XXV, XXIV D 5	XXIV F 5	XXII B 5
[25] XXV F 6	XXIII B 6	[25] XXV B 6	XXIII E 6	XXIII G 6	XXI C 6
XXIV G 7	XXII C 7	XXIV C 7	XXII F 7	XXII A 7	XX D 7
XXIII A 8	XXI D 8	XXIII D 8	XXI G 8	XXI B 8	XIX E 8
XXII B 9	XX E 9	XXII E 9	XX A 9	XX C 9	XVIII F 9
XXI C 10	XIX F 10	XXI F 10	XIX B 10	XIX D 10	XVII G 10
XX D 11	XVIII G 11	XX G 11	XVIII C 11	XVIII E 11	XVI A 11
XIX E 12	XVII A 12	XIX A 12	XVII D 12	XVII F 12	XV B 12
XVIII F 13	XVI B 13	XVIII B 13	XVI E 13	XVI G 13	XIV C 13
XVII G 14	XV C 14	XVII C 14	XV F 14	XV A 14	XIII D 14
XVI A 15	XIV D 15	XVI D 15	XIV G 15	XIV B 15	XII E 15
XV B 16	XIII E 16	XV E 16	XIII A 16	XIII C 16	XI F 16
XIV C 17	XII F 17	XIV F 17	XII B 17	XII D 17	X G 17
XIII D 18	XI G 18	XIII G 18	XI C 18	XI E 18	IX A 18
XII E 19	X A 19	XII A 19	X D 19	X F 19	VIII B 19
XI F 20	IX B 20	XI B 20	IX E 20	IX G 20	VII C 20
X G 21	VIII C 21	X C 21	VIII F 21	VIII A 21	VI D 21
IX A 22	VII D 22	IX D 22	VII G 22	VII B 22	V E 22
VIII B 23	VI E 23	VIII E 23	VI A 23	VI C 23	IV F 23
VII C 24	V F 24	VII F 24	V B 24	V D 24	III G 24
VI D 25	IV G 25	VI G 25	IV C 25	IV E 25	II A 25
V E 26	III A 26	V A 26	III D 26	III F 26	I B 26
IV F 27	II B 27	IV B 27	II E 27	II G 27	* C 27
III G 28	I C 28	III C 28	I F 28	I A 28	XXIX D 28
II A 29		II D 29	* G 29	* B 29	XXVIII E 29
I B 30		I E 30	XXIX A 30	XXIX C 30	XXVII F 30
* C 31		* F 31		XXVIII D 31	

Explanation in *Section 11*.

TABLE IX

New Style Yearly Calendar

July Epact	DL	August		September		October		November		December	
XXVI	G 1	XXV, XXIV	C 1	XXIII	F 1	XXII	A 1	XXI	D 1	XX	F 1
[25] XXV	A 2	XXIII	D 2	XXII	G 2	XXI	B 2	XX	E 2	XIX	G 2
XXIV	B 3	XXII	E 3	XXI	A 3	XX	C 3	XIX	F 3	XVIII	A 3
XXIII	C 4	XXI	F 4	XX	B 4	XIX	D 4	XVIII	G 4	XVII	B 4
XXII	D 5	XX	G 5	XIX	C 5	XVIII	E 5	XVII	A 5	XVI	C 5
XXI	E 6	XIX	A 6	XVIII	D 6	XVII	F 6	XVI	B 6	XV	D 6
XX	F 7	XVIII	B 7	XVII	E 7	XVI	G 7	XV	C 7	XIV	E 7
XIX	G 8	XVII	C 8	XVI	F 8	XV	A 8	XIV	D 8	XIII	F 8
XVIII	A 9	XVI	D 9	XV	G 9	XIV	B 9	XIII	E 9	XII	G 9
XVII	B 10	XV	E 10	XIV	A 10	XIII	C 10	XII	F 10	XI	A 10
XVI	C 11	XIV	F 11	XIII	B 11	XII	D 11	XI	G 11	X	B 11
XV	D 12	XIII	G 12	XII	C 12	XI	E 12	X	A 12	IX	C 12
XIV	E 13	XII	A 13	XI	D 13	X	F 13	IX	B 13	VIII	D 13
XIII	F 14	XI	B 14	X	E 14	IX	G 14	VIII	C 14	VII	E 14
XII	G 15	X	C 15	IX	F 15	VIII	A 15	VII	D 15	VI	F 15
XI	A 16	IX	D 16	VIII	G 16	VII	B 16	VI	E 16	V	G 16
X	B 17	VIII	E 17	VII	A 17	VI	C 17	V	F 17	IV	A 17
IX	C 18	VII	F 18	VI	B 18	V	D 18	IV	G 18	III	B 18
VIII	D 19	VI	G 19	V	C 19	IV	E 19	III	A 19	II	C 19
VII	E 20	V	A 20	IV	D 20	III	F 20	II	B 20	I	D 20
VI	F 21	IV	B 21	III	E 21	II	G 21	I	C 21	*	E 21
V	G 22	III	C 22	II	F 22	I	A 22	*	D 22	XXIX	F 22
IV	A 23	II	D 23	I	G 23	*	B 23	XXIX	E 23	XXVIII	G 23
III	B 24	I	E 24	*	A 24	XXIX	C 24	XXVIII	F 24	XXVII	A 24
II	C 25	*	F 25	XXIX	B 25	XXVIII	D 25	XXVII	G 25	XXVI	B 25
I	D 26	XXIX	G 26	XXVIII	C 26	XXVII	E 26	[25] XXVI	A 26	[25] XXV	C 26
*	E 27	XXVIII	A 27	XXVII	D 27	XXVI	F 27	XXV, XXIV	B 27	XXIV	D 27
XXIX	F 28	XXVII	B 28	[25] XXVI	E 28	[25] XXV	G 28	XXIII	C 28	XXIII	E 28
XXVIII	G 29	XXVI	C 29	XXV, XXIV	F 29	XXIV	A 29	XXII	D 29	XXII	F 29
XXVII	A 30	[25] XXV	D 30	XXIII	G 30	XXIII	B 30	XXI	E 30	XXI	G 30
[25] XXVI	B 31	XXIV	E 31			XXII	C 31			[19] XX	A 31

TABLE X

Old Paschal Table, Reformed

Epact	Easter New Moon	14th Moon	DL	Sept. Sun	Ash Wed	East. Sun	Asc. Thu	Pent. Sun	Corp. Chris.	Adv. Sun
XXIII	Mar 8 + 13 =	Mar 21	C							
XXII	Mar 9	Mar 22	D	Jan 18	Feb 4	Mar 22	Apr 30	May 10	May 21	Nov 29
XXI	Mar 10	Mar 23	E	19	5	23	May 1	11	22	30
XX	Mar 11	Mar 24	F	20	6	24	2	12	23	Dec 1
XIX	Mar 12	Mar 25	G	21	7	25	3	13	24	2
XVIII	Mar 13	Mar 26	A	22	8	26	4	14	25	3
XVII	Mar 14	Mar 27	B	23	9	27	5	15	26	Nov 27
XVI	Mar 15	Mar 28	C	24	10	28	6	16	27	28
XV	Mar 16	Mar 29	D	25	11	29	7	17	28	29
XIV	Mar 17	Mar 30	E	26	12	30	8	18	29	30
XIII	Mar 18	Mar 31	F	27	13	31	9	19	30	Dec 1
XII	Mar 19	Apr 1	G	28	14	Apr 1	10	20	31	2
XI	Mar 20	Apr 2	A	29	15	2	11	21	Jun 1	3
X	Mar 21	Apr 3	B	30	16	3	12	22	2	Nov 27
IX	Mar 22	Apr 4	C	31	17	4	13	23	3	28
VIII	Mar 23	Apr 5	D	Feb 1	18	5	14	24	4	29
VII	Mar 24	Apr 6	E	2	19	6	15	25	5	30
VI	Mar 25	Apr 7	F	3	20	7	16	26	6	Dec 1
V	Mar 26	Apr 8	G	4	21	8	17	27	7	2
IV	Mar 27	Apr 9	A	5	22	9	18	28	8	3
III	Mar 28	Apr 10	B	6	23	10	19	29	9	Nov 27
II	Mar 29	Apr 11	C	7	24	11	20	30	10	28
I	Mar 30	Apr 12	D	8	25	12	21	31	11	29
*	Mar 31	Apr 13	E	9	26	13	22	Jun 1	12	30
XXIX	Apr 1	Apr 14	F	10	27	14	23	2	13	Dec 1
XXVIII	Apr 2	Apr 15	G	11	28	15	24	3	14	2
XXVII	Apr 3	Apr 16	A	12	Mar 1	16	25	4	15	3
[25] XXVI	Apr 4	Apr 17	B	13	2	17	26	5	16	Nov 27
XXV, XXIV	Apr 5	Apr 18	C	14	3	18	27	6	17	28
			D	15	4	19	28	7	18	29
			E	16	5	20	29	8	19	30
			F	17	6	21	30	9	20	Dec 1
			G	18	7	22	31	10	21	2
			A	19	8	23	Jun 1	11	22	3
			B	20	9	24	2	12	23	Nov 27
			C	21	10	25	3	13	24	28

Explanation in *Section 15*.

TABLE XI

New Reformed Paschal Table

DL	Epacts	Sept. Sun	Ash Wed	East. Sun	Asc. Thu	Pent. Sun	Corp. Chris.	Adv. Sun
	XXIII	Jan 18	Feb 4	Mar 22	Apr 30	May 10	May 21	
	XXII, XXI......XVI	Jan 25	Feb 11	Mar 29	May 7	May 17	May 28	
D	XV, XIV.........IX	Feb 1	Feb 18	Apr 5	May 14	May 24	Jun 4	Nov 29
	VIII, VII.........II	Feb 8	Feb 25	Apr 12	May 21	May 31	Jun 11	
	I, *.............XXIV	Feb 15	Mar 4	Apr 19	May 28	Jun 7	Jun 18	
	XXIII, XXII	Jan 19	Feb 5	Mar 23	May 1	May 11	May 22	
	XXI, XX........XV	Jan 26	Feb 12	Mar 30	May 8	May 18	May 29	
E	XIV, XIII.......VIII	Feb 2	Feb 19	Apr 6	May 15	May 25	Jun 5	Nov 30
	VII, VI..........I	Feb 9	Feb 26	Apr 13	May 22	Jun 1	Jun 12	
	*, XXIX........XXIV	Feb 16	Mar 5	Apr 20	May 29	Jun 8	Jun 19	
	XXIII, XXII....XXI	Jan 20	Feb 6	Mar 24	May 2	May 12	May 23	
	XX, XIX........XIV	Jan 27	Feb 13	Mar 31	May 9	May 19	May 30	
F	XIII, XII........VII	Feb 3	Feb 20	Apr 7	May 16	May 26	Jun 6	Dec 1
	VI, V...........*	Feb 10	Feb 27	Apr 14	May 23	Jun 2	Jun 13	
	XXIX, XXVIII..XXIV	Feb 17	Mar 6	Apr 21	May 30	Jun 9	Jun 20	
	XXIII, XXIII....XX	Jan 21	Feb 7	Mar 25	May 3	May 13	May 24	
	XIX, XVIII......XIII	Jan 28	Feb 14	Apr 1	May 10	May 20	May 31	
G	XII, XI..........VI	Feb 4	Feb 21	Apr 8	May 17	May 27	Jun 7	Dec 2
	V, IV............XXIX	Feb 11	Feb 28	Apr 15	May 24	Jun 3	Jun 14	
	XXVIII, XXVII..XXIV	Feb 18	Mar 7	Apr 22	May 31	Jun 10	Jun 21	
	XXIII, XXII.....XIX	Jan 22	Feb 8	Mar 26	May 4	May 14	May 25	
	XVIII, XVII.....XII	Jan 29	Feb 15	Apr 2	May 11	May 21	Jun 1	
A	XI, X............V	Feb 5	Feb 22	Apr 9	May 18	May 28	Jun 8	Dec 3
	IV, III...........XXVIII	Feb 12	Mar 1	Apr 16	May 25	Jun 4	Jun 15	
	XXVII, XXVI...XXIV	Feb 19	Mar 8	Apr 23	Jun 1	Jun 11	Jun 22	
	XXIII, XXII....XVIII	Jan 23	Feb 9	Mar 27	May 5	May 15	May 26	
	XVII, XVI.......XI	Jan 30	Feb 16	Apr 3	May 12	May 22	Jun 2	
B	X, IX............IV	Feb 6	Feb 23	Apr 10	May 19	May 29	Jun 9	Nov 27
	III, II............XXVII	Feb 13	Mar 2	Apr 17	May 26	Jun 5	Jun 16	
	XXVI, [25].......XXIV	Feb 20	Mar 9	Apr 24	Jun 2	Jun 12	Jun 23	
	XXIII, XXII....XVII	Jan 24	Feb 10	Mar 28	May 6	May 16	May 27	
	XVI, XV.........X	Jan 31	Feb 17	Apr 4	May 13	May 23	Jun 3	
C	IX, VIII.........III	Feb 7	Feb 24	Apr 11	May 20	May 30	Jun 10	Nov 28
	II, I.............[25]	Feb 14	Mar 3	Apr 18	May 27	Jun 6	Jun 17	
	XXV, XXIV	Feb 21	Mar 10	Apr 25	Jun 3	Jun 13	Jun 24	

Explanation in *Section 15.*

TABLE XII

Old Style 19-year Cycle of New Moon Dates

(Used before AD 1582.)

GN	Epacts													
1	XI	Mar 23 29	Apr 21 30	May 21 29	Jun 19 30	Jul 19 29	Aug 17 30	Sep 16 29	Oct 15 30	Nov 14 29	Dec 13 30	Jan 12 29	Feb 10 30	
2	XXII	Mar 12 29	Apr 10 30	May 10 29	Jun 8 30	Jul 8 29	Aug 6 30	Sep 5 29	Oct 4 30	Nov 3 29	Dec 2 30	Jan 1 29	Jan 30 30	
3	III	Mar 1 □	Mar 31 29	Apr 29 30	May 29 29	Jun 27 30	Jul 27 29	Aug 25 30	Sep 24 29	Oct 23 30	Nov 22 29	Dec 21 30	Jan 20 29	Feb 18 30
4	XIV	Mar 20 29	Apr 18 30	May 18 29	Jun 16 30	Jul 16 29	Aug 14 30	Sep 13 29	Oct 12 30	Nov 11 29	Dec 10 30	Jan 9 29	Feb 7 30	
5	XXV	Mar 9 29	Apr 7 30	May 7 29	Jun 5 30	Jul 5 29	Aug 3 30	Sep 2 29	Oct 1 30	Oct 31 29	Nov 29 30	Dec 29 29	Jan 27 30	Feb 26 □
6	VI	Mar 28 29	Apr 26 30	May 26 29	Jun 24 30	Jul 24 29	Aug 22 30	Sep 21 29	Oct 20 30	Nov 19 29	Dec 18 30	Jan 17 29	Feb 15 30	
7	XVII	Mar 17 29	Apr 15 30	May 15 29	Jun 13 30	Jul 13 29	Aug 11 30	Sep 10 29	Oct 9 30	Nov 8 29	Dec 7 30	Jan 6 29	Feb 4 30	
8	XXVIII	Mar 6 □	Apr 5 29	May 4 30	Jun 3 29	Jul 2 30	Aug 1 29	Aug 30 30	Sep 29 29	Oct 28 30	Nov 27 29	Dec 26 30	Jan 25 29	Feb 23 30
9	IX	Mar 25 29	Apr 23 30	May 23 29	Jun 21 30	Jul 21 29	Aug 19 30	Sep 18 29	Oct 17 30	Nov 16 29	Dec 15 30	Jan 14 29	Feb 12 30	
10	XX	Mar 14 29	Apr 12 30	May 12 29	Jun 10 30	Jul 10 29	Aug 8 30	Sep 7 29	Oct 6 30	Nov 5 29	Dec 4 30	Jan 3 29	Feb 1 30	
11	I	Mar 3 □	Apr 2 29	May 1 30	May 31 29	Jun 29 30	Jul 29 29	Aug 27 30	Sep 26 29	Oct 25 30	Nov 24 29	Dec 23 30	Jan 22 29	Feb 20 30
12	XII	Mar 22 29	Apr 20 30	May 20 29	Jun 18 30	Jul 18 29	Aug 16 30	Sep 15 29	Oct 14 30	Nov 13 29	Dec 12 30	Jan 11 29	Feb 9 30	
13	XXIII	Mar 11 29	Apr 9 30	May 9 29	Jun 7 30	Jul 7 29	Aug 5 30	Sep 4 29	Oct 3 30	Nov 2 29	Dec 1 30	Dec 31 29	Jan 29 30	Feb 28 □

14	IV	Mar. 30 29	Apr 28 30	May 28 29	Jun 26 30	Jul 26 29	Aug 24 30	Sep 23 29	Oct 22 30	Nov 21 29	Dec 20 30	Jan 19 29	Feb 17 30	
15	XV	Mar 19 29	Apr 17 30	May 17 29	Jun 15 30	Jul 15 29	Aug 13 30	Sep 12 29	Oct 11 30	Nov 10 29	Dec 9 30	Jan 8 29	Feb 6 30	
16	XXVI	Mar 8 29	Apr 6 30	May 6 29	Jun 4 30	Jul 4 29	Aug 2 30	Sep 1 29	Sep 30 30	Oct 30 29	Nov 28 30	Dec 28 29	Jan 26 30	Feb25 □
17	VII	Mar 27 29	Apr 25 30	May 25 29	Jun 23 30	Jul 23 29	Aug 21 30	Sep 20 29	Oct 19 30	Nov 18 29	Dec 17 30	Jan 16 29	Feb 14 30	
18	XVIII	Mar 16 29	Apr 14 30	May 14 29	Jun 12 30	Jul 12 29	Aug 10 30	Sep 9 29	Oct 8 30	Nov 7 29	Dec 6 30	Jan 5 29	Feb 3 30	
19	XXIX +XII	Mar 5 □	Apr 4 29	May 3 30	Jun 2 29	Jul 1 30	Jul 31 29	Aug 29 30	Sep 28 29	Oct 27 30	Nov 26 29	Dec 25 30	Jan 24 29	Feb22 (30–1)
1	XI	Mar 23 etc.												

The symbol □ means (29½ + ½) or 30 days.

Explanation in *Section 16*.

TABLE XIII

Old Style Yearly Calendar

(Used before AD 1582)

FIRST HALF YEAR

GN	March Ep	DL		April				May				June				July				August			
3	III	D	1			G	1	11	I	B	1			E	1	19	XXIX	G	1	8	XXVIII	C	1
		E	2	11	I	A	2			C	2	19	XXIX	F	2	8	XXVIII	A	2	16	XXVI	D	2
11	I	F	3			B	3	19	XXIX	D	3	8	XXVIII	G	3			B	3	5	XXV	E	3
		G	4	19	XXIX	C	4	8	XXVIII	E	4	16	XXVI	A	4	16	XXVI	C	4			F	4
19	XXIX	A	5	8	XXVIII	D	5			F	5	5	XXV	B	5	5	XXV	D	5	13	XXIII	G	5
8	XXVIII	B	6	16	XXVI	E	6	16	XXVI	G	6			C	6			E	6	2	XXII	A	6
		C	7	5	XXV	F	7	5	XXV	A	7	13	XXIII	D	7	13	XXIII	F	7			B	7
16	XXVI	D	8			G	8			B	8	2	XXII	E	8	2	XXII	G	8	10	XX	C	8
5	XXV	E	9	13	XXIII	A	9	13	XXIII	C	9			F	9			A	9			D	9
		F	10	2	XXII	B	10	2	XXII	D	10	10	XX	G	10	10	XX	B	10	18	XVIII	E	10
13	XXIII	G	11			C	11			E	11			A	11			C	11	7	XVII	F	11
2	XXII	A	12	10	XX	D	12	10	XX	F	12	18	XVIII	B	12	18	XVIII	D	12			G	12
		B	13			E	13			G	13	7	XVII	C	13	7	XVII	E	13	15	XV	A	13
10	XX	C	14	18	XVIII	F	14	18	XVIII	A	14			D	14			F	14	4	XIV	B	14
		D	15	7	XVII	G	15	7	XVII	B	15	15	XV	E	15	15	XV	G	15			C	15
18	XVIII	E	16			A	16			C	16	4	XIV	F	16	4	XIV	A	16	12	XII	D	16
7	XVII	F	17	15	XV	B	17	15	XV	D	17			G	17			B	17	1	XI	E	17
		G	18	4	XIV	C	18	4	XIV	E	18	12	XII	A	18	12	XII	C	18			F	18
15	XV	A	19			D	19			F	19	1	XI	B	19	1	XI	D	19	9	IX	G	19
4	XIV	B	20	12	XII	E	20	12	XII	G	20			C	20			E	20			A	20
		C	21	1	XI	F	21	1	XI	A	21	9	IX	D	21	9	IX	F	21	17	VII	B	21
12	XII	D	22			G	22			B	22			E	22			G	22	6	VI	C	22
1	XI	E	23	9	IX	A	23	9	IX	C	23	17	VII	F	23	17	VII	A	23			D	23
		F	24			B	24			D	24	6	VI	G	24	6	VI	B	24	14	IV	E	24
9	IX	G	25	17	VII	C	25	17	VII	E	25			A	25			C	25	3	III	F	25
		A	26	6	VI	D	26	6	VI	F	26	14	IV	B	26	14	IV	D	26			G	26
17	VII	B	27			E	27			G	27	3	III	C	27	3	III	E	27	11	I	A	27
6	VI	C	28	14	IV	F	28	14	IV	A	28			D	28			F	28			B	28
		D	29	3	III	G	29	3	III	B	29	11	I	E	29	11	I	G	29	19	XXIX	C	29
14	IV	E	30			A	30			C	30			F	30			A	30	8	XXVIII	D	30
3	III	F	31					11	I	D	31					19	XXIX	B	31			E	31

Explanation in *Section 16*.

TABLE XIII

Old Style Yearly Calendar

SECOND HALF YEAR

September				October				November				December				January				February			
GN	Ep	DL																					
16	XXVI	F	1	5	XXV	A	1			D	1	13	XXIII	F	1	2	XXII	B	1	10	XX	E	1
5	XXV	G	2			B	2	13	XXIII	E	2	2	XXII	G	2			C	2			F	2
		A	3	13	XXIII	C	3	2	XXII	F	3			A	3	10	XX	D	3	18	XVIII	G	3
13	XXIII	B	4	2	XXII	D	4			G	4	10	XX	B	4			E	4	7	XVII	A	4
2	XXII	C	5			E	5	10	XX	A	5			C	5	18	XVIII	F	5			B	5
		D	6	10	XX	F	6			B	6	18	XVIII	D	6	7	XVII	G	6	15	XV	C	6
10	XX	E	7			G	7	18	XVIII	C	7	7	XVII	E	7			A	7	4	XIV	D	7
		F	8	18	XVIII	A	8	7	XVII	D	8			F	8	15	XV	B	8			E	8
18	XVIII	G	9	7	XVII	B	9			E	9	15	XV	G	9	4	XIV	C	9	12	XII	F	9
7	XVII	A	10			C	10	15	XV	F	10	4	XIV	A	10			D	10	1	XI	G	10
		B	11	15	XV	D	11	4	XIV	G	11			B	11	12	XII	E	11			A	11
15	XV	C	12	4	XIV	E	12			A	12	12	XII	C	12	1	XI	F	12	9	IX	B	12
4	XIV	D	13			F	13	12	XII	B	13	1	XI	D	13			G	13			C	13
		E	14	12	XII	G	14	1	XI	C	14			E	14	9	IX	A	14	17	VII	D	14
12	XII	F	15	1	XI	A	15			D	15	9	IX	F	15			B	15	6	VI	E	15
1	XI	G	16			B	16	9	IX	E	16			G	16	17	VII	C	16			F	16
		A	17	9	IX	C	17			F	17	17	VII	A	17	6	VI	D	17	14	IV	G	17
9	IX	B	18			D	18	17	VII	G	18	6	VI	B	18			E	18	3	III	A	18
		C	19	17	VII	E	19	6	VI	A	19			C	19	14	IV	F	19			B	19
17	VII	D	20	6	VI	F	20			B	20	14	IV	D	20	3	III	G	20	11	I	C	20
6	VI	E	21			G	21	14	IV	C	21	3	III	E	21			A	21			D	21
		F	22	14	IV	A	22	3	III	D	22			F	22	11	I	B	22	19	XXIX	E	22
14	IV	G	23	3	III	B	23			E	23	11	I	G	23			C	23	8	XXVIII	F	23
3	III	A	24			C	24	11	I	F	24			A	24	19	XXIX	D	24			G	24
		B	25	11	I	D	25			G	25	19	XXIX	B	25	8	XXVIII	E	25	16	XXVI	A	25
11	I	C	26			E	26	19	XXIX	A	26	8	XXVIII	C	26	16	XXVI	F	26	5	XXV	B	26
		D	27	19	XXIX	F	27	8	XXVIII	B	27			D	27	5	XXV	G	27			C	27
19	XXIX	E	28	8	XXVIII	G	28	16	XXVI	C	28	16	XXVI	E	28			A	28	13	XXIII	D	28
8	XXVIII	F	29			A	29	5	XXV	D	29	5	XXV	F	29	13	XXIII	B	29				
16	XXVI	G	30	16	XXVI	B	30			E	30			G	30	2	XXII	C	30				
				5	XXV	C	31					13	XXIII	A	31			D	31				

TABLE XIV
Old Style Paschal Table
(Used before AD 1582)

GN	Trad. Epacts	East. New Moon	East. Full Moon	DL	Sept. Sun	Ash Wed	East. Sun	Asc. Thu	Pent. Sun	Corp. Chr.	Adv. Sun
16	XXVI	Mar 8 + 13 =	Mar 21	C							
5	XXV	9	22	D	Jan 18	Feb 4	Mar 22	Apr 30	May 10	May 21	Nov 29
		10	23	E	19	5	23	May 1	11	22	30
13	XXIII	11	24	F	20	6	24	2	12	23	Dec 1
2	XXII	12	25	G	21	7	25	3	13	24	2
		13	26	A	22	8	26	4	14	25	3
10	XX	14	27	B	23	9	27	5	15	26	Nov 27
		15	28	C	24	10	28	6	16	27	28
18	XVIII	16	29	D	25	11	29	7	17	28	29
7	XVII	17	30	E	26	12	30	8	18	29	30
		18	31	F	27	13	31	9	19	30	Dec 1
15	XV	19	Apr 1	G	28	14	Apr 1	10	20	31	2
4	XIV	20	2	A	29	15	2	11	21	Jun 1	3
		21	3	B	30	16	3	12	22	2	Nov 27
12	XII	22	4	C	31	17	4	13	23	3	28
1	XI	23	5	D	Feb 1	18	5	14	24	4	29
		24	6	E	2	19	6	15	25	5	30
9	IX	25	7	F	3	20	7	16	26	6	Dec 1
		26	8	G	4	21	8	17	27	7	2

17	VII	27	9	A	5	22	9	18	28	8	3
6	VI	28	10	B	6	23	10	19	29	9	Nov 27
		29	11	C	7	24	11	20	30	10	28
14	IV	30	12	D	8	25	12	21	31	11	29
3	III	31	13	E	9	26	13	22	Jun 1	12	30
		Apr 1	14	F	10	27	14	23	2	13	Dec 1
11	I	2	15	G	11	28	15	24	3	14	2
		3	16	A	12	Mar 1	16	25	4	15	3
19	XXIX	4	17	B	13	2	17	26	5	16	Nov 27
8	XXVIII	Apr 5	Apr 18	C	14	3	18	27	6	17	28
				D	15	4	19	28	7	18	29
				E	16	5	20	29	8	19	30
				F	17	6	21	30	9	20	Dec 1
				G	18	7	22	31	10	21	2
				A	19	8	23	Jun 1	11	22	3
				B	20	9	24	2	12	23	Nov 27
				C	Feb 21	Mar 10	Apr 25	Jun 3	Jun 13	Jun 24	28

Explanation in *Section 16.*

TABLE XV

Easter New Moon Dates at 19-Year Intervals

(AD 1583 to 4414)

Year	Mean E.N.M.	Epact (GN = 7)	Cal. E.N.M.	L	Year	Mean E.N.M.	Epact (GN = 7)	Cal. E.N.M.	L	Year	Mean E.N.M.	Epact (GN = 7)	Cal. E.N.M.	L
1583	Mar 23.84	VII	Mar 24	1	2533	Mar 27.24	III	Mar 28	1	3483	Mar 31.65	XXIX	Mar 32	1
1602	23.52			1	52	26.93			2	3502	32.34	XXVIII	Mar 33	1
21	23.21			1	71	27.62			1	21	32.03			1
40	22.90			2	90	27.31			1	40	31.72			2
59	23.59			1	2609	28.00	II	Mar 29	1	59	32.41			1
78	23.28			1	28	27.69			2	78	32.09			1
97	22.96			2	47	28.37			1	97	31.78			2
1716	23.65	VI	Mar 25	2	66	28.06			1	3616	31.47	XXIX	Mar 32	1
35	24.34			1	85	27.75			2	35	32.16			0
54	24.03			1	2704	28.44			1	54	31.85			1
73	23.72			2	23	29.13			0	73	31.54			1
92	23.41			2	42	28.81			1	92	31.22			1
1811	25.09			0	61	28.50			1	3711	32.91	XXVIII	Mar 33	1
30	24.78			1	80	28.19			1	30	32.60			1
49	24.47			1	99	28.88			1	49	32.29			1
68	24.16			1	2818	28.57			1	68	31.98			2
87	24.85			1	37	28.26			1	87	32.66			1
1906	25.53	V	Mar 26	1	56	27.94			2	3806	33.35	XXVII	Mar 34	1
25	25.22			1	75	28.63			1	25	33.04			1
44	24.91			2	94	28.32			1	44	32.73			2
63	25.60			1	2913	29.01	I	Mar 30	1	63	33.42			1
82	25.29			1	32	28.70			2	82	33.11			1
2001	24.98			2	51	29.38			1	3901	33.79			1
20	24.66			2	70	29.07			1	20	33.48			1
39	25.35			1	89	28.76			2	39	34.17			0
58	25.04			1	3008	29.45			1	58	33.86			1
77	24.73			2	27	30.14			0	77	33.55			1

96	24.42			2	46	29.83			1	96	33.23			1
2115	26.10			0	65	29.51			1	4015	33.92			1
34	25.79			1	84	29.20			1	34	33.61			1
53	25.48			1	3103	30.89	*	Mar 31	1	53	33.30			1
72	25.17			1	22	30.58			1	72	32.99			2
91	25.86			1	41	30.27			1	91	33.68			1
2210	26.55	IV	Mar 27	1	60	29.95			2	4110	34.36	XXVI	Mar 35	1
29	26.23			1	79	30.64			1	29	34.05			1
48	25.92			2	98	30.33			1	48	33.74			2
67	26.61			1	3217	30.02			1	67	34.43			1
86	26.30			1	36	29.71			2	86	34.12			1
2305	26.99	III	Mar 28	2	55	30.40			1	4205	34.80	XXV	Mar 36	2
24	26.67			2	74	30.08			1	24	34.49			2
43	27.36			1	93	29.77			2	43	35.18			1
62	27.05			1	3312	30.46			1	62	34.87			2
81	26.74			2	31	31.15			0	81	34.56			2
2400	26.43	IV	Mar 27	1	50	30.84			1	4300	35.25			1
19	27.12			0	69	30.52			1	19	35.93			1
38	26.80			1	88	30.21			1	38	35.62			1
57	26.49			1	3407	31.90	XXIX	Mar 32	1	57	35.31			1
76	26.18			1	26	31.59			1	76	35.00			1
95	26.87			1	45	31.28			1	95	35.69			1
2514	27.56	III	Mar 28	1	64	30.97			2	4414	35.37			1

Explanation in *Section 22*.

TABLE XVI

Easter New Moon Dates, Annual

(AD 1928 to 2071)

Year	Mean E.N.M.	G.N. Ep.	Cal. E.N.M.	L	Year	Mean E.N.M.	G.N. Ep.	Cal. E.N.M.	L	Year	Mean E.N.M.	G.N. Ep.	Cal. E.N.M.	L
1928	Mar 21.85	10 VIII	Mar 23	2	1976	Mar 31.03	1 XXIX	Mar 32	1	2024	Mar 10.66	11 XIX	Mar 12	2
29	11.22	11 XIX	12	1	77	20.39	2 X	21	1	25	29.56	12 *	31	2
30	30.12	12 *	31	1	78	9.76	3 XXI	10	1	26	18.93	13 XI	20	2
31	19.49	13 XI	20	1	79	28.66	4 II	29	1	27	8.30	14 XXII	9	1
32	7.85	14 XXII	9	2	80	17.02	5 XIII	18	1	28	26.19	15 III	28	2
33	26.75	15 III	28	2	81	35.92	6 XXIV	36	1	29	15.56	16 XIV	17	2
34	16.12	16 XIV	17	1	82	25.29	7 V	26	1	30	34.46	17 [25]	35	1
35	35.02	17 [25]	35	0	83	14.65	8 XVI	15	1	31	23.83	18 VI	25	2
36	23.38	18 VI	25	2	84	32.55	9 XXVII	34	2	32	12.19	19 XVII	14	2
37	12.75	19 XVII	14	2	85	21.92	10 VIII	23	2	33	31.09	1 XXIX	32	1
38	31.65	1 XXIX	32	1	86	11.29	11 XIX	12	1	34	20.46	2 X	21	1
39	21.02	2 X	21	0	87	30.18	12 *	31	1	35	9.82	3 XXI	10	1
40	9.38	3 XXI	10	1	88	18.55	13 XI	20	2	36	27.72	4 II	29	2
41	28.28	4 II	29	1	89	7.92	14 XXII	9	2	37	17.09	5 XIII	18	1
42	17.65	5 XIII	18	1	90	26.82	15 III	28	2	38	35.99	6 XXIV	36	1
43	36.55	6 XXIV	36	0	91	16.18	16 XIV	17	1	39	25.35	7 V	26	1
44	24.91	7 V	26	2	92	34.08	17 [25]	35	1	40	13.72	8 XVI	15	2
45	14.28	8 XVI	15	1	93	23.45	18 VI	25	2	41	32.62	9 XXVII	34	2
46	33.18	9 XXVII	34	1	94	12.82	19 XVII	14	2	42	21.98	10 VIII	23	2
47	22.54	10 VIII	23	1	95	31.71	1 XXIX	32	1	43	11.35	11 XIX	12	1
48	10.91	11 XIX	12	2	96	20.08	2 X	21	1	44	29.25	12 *	31	2
49	29.81	12 *	31	2	97	9.45	3 XXI	10	1	45	18.62	13 XI	20	2
50	19.18	13 XI	20	1	98	28.35	4 II	29	1	46	7.98	14 XXII	9	2
51	8.54	14 XXII	9	1	99	17.71	5 XIII	18	1	47	26.88	15 III	28	2

52	26.44	15	III	28	2	2000	35.61	6	XXIV	36	1	48	15.25	16	XIV	17	2
53	15.81	16	XIV	17	2	1	24.98	7	V	26	2	49	34.15	17	[25]	35	1
54	34.71	17	[25]	35	1	2	14.34	8	XVI	15	1	50	23.51	18	VI	25	2
55	24.07	18	VI	25	1	3	33.24	9	XXVII	34	1	51	12.88	19	XVII	14	2
56	12.44	19	XVII	14	2	4	21.61	10	VIII	23	2	52	30.78	1	XXIX	32	2
57	31.34	1	XXIX	32	1	5	10.97	11	XIX	12	2	53	20.15	2	X	21	1
58	20.70	2	X	21	1	6	29.87	12	*	31	2	54	9.51	3	XXI	10	1
59	10.07	3	XXI	10	0	7	19.24	13	XI	20	1	55	28.41	4	II	29	1
60	27.97	4	II	29	2	8	7.61	14	XXII	9	2	56	16.78	5	XIII	18	2
61	17.34	5	XIII	18	1	9	26.50	15	III	28	2	57	35.68	6	XXIV	36	1
62	36.23	6	XXIV	36	0	10	15.87	16	XIV	17	2	58	25.04	7	V	26	1
63	25.60	7	V	26	1	11	34.77	17	[25]	35	1	59	14.41	8	XVI	15	1
64	13.97	8	XVI	15	2	12	23.14	18	VI	25	2	60	32.31	9	XXVII	34	2
65	32.87	9	XXVII	34	2	13	12.50	19	XVII	14	2	61	21.67	10	VIII	23	2
66	22.23	10	VIII	23	1	14	31.40	1	XXIX	32	1	62	11.04	11	XIX	12	1
67	11.60	11	XIX	12	1	15	20.77	2	X	21	1	63	29.94	12	*	31	2
68	29.50	12	*	31	2	16	9.14	3	XXI	10	1	64	18.30	13	XI	20	2
69	18.86	13	XI	20	2	17	28.03	4	II	29	1	65	7.67	14	XXII	9	2
70	8.23	14	XXII	9	1	18	17.40	5	XIII	18	1	66	26.57	15	III	28	2
71	27.13	15	III	28	1	19	36.30	6	XXIV	36	0	67	15.94	16	XIV	17	2
72	15.50	16	XIV	17	2	20	24.66	7	V	26	2	68	33.83	17	[25]	35	2
73	34.39	17	[25]	35	1	21	14.03	8	XVI	15	1	69	23.20	18	VI	25	2
74	23.76	18	VI	25	2	22	32.93	9	XXVII	34	2	70	12.57	19	XVII	14	2
75	13.13	19	XVII	14	1	23	22.30	10	VIII	23	1	71	31.47	1	XXIX	32	1

Explanation in *Section 22.*

TABLE XVII

Construction of Universal Paschal Table without Epacts

Easter New Moon Dates	AD 0–1582	1582–1699	1700–1899	1900–2199	2200–2299	2300–2399	2400–2499	2500–2599	2600–2899	2900–3099	3100–3399
	A	B	C	D	E	F	M	N		H	I
Mar 8	16	3	14		6	17	6	17		9	
Mar 9	5		3	14		6		6	17		9
Mar 10		11		3	14		14		6	17	
Mar 11	13		11		3	14	3	14		6	17
Mar 12	2	19		11		3		3	14		6
Mar 13		8	19		11		11		3	14	
Mar 14	10		8	19		11		11		3	14
Mar 15		16		8	19		19		11		3
Mar 16	18	5	16		8	19	8	19		11	
Mar 17	7		5	16		8		8	19		11
Mar 18		13		5	16		16		8	19	
Mar 19	15	2	13		5	16	5	16		8	19
Mar 20	4		2	13		5		5	16		8
Mar 21		10		2	13		13		5	16	
Mar 22	12		10		2	13	2	13		5	16
Mar 23	1	18		10		2		2	13		5
Mar 24		7	18		10		10		2	13	
Mar 25	9		7	18		10		10		2	13
Mar 26		15		7	18		18		10		2
Mar 27	17	4	15		7	18	7	18		10	
Mar 28	6		4	15		7		7	18		10
Mar 29		12		4	15		15		7	18	
Mar 30	14	1	12		4	15	4	15		7	18
Mar 31	3		1	12		4		4	15		7
Apr 1		9		1	12		12		4	15	
Apr 2	11		9		1	12	1	12		4	15
Apr 3		17		9		1		1	12		4
Apr 4	19	6	17		9		9		1	12	
	8		6	17		9		9		1	12
Apr 5		14		6	17		17		9		1

Explanation in *Section 28.*

TABLE XVIII

Universal Paschal Table without Epacts

AD 0–1582 GN	1583–1699	1700–1899	1900–2199	2200–2299 / 2400–2499	2300–2399 / 2500–2599	2600–2899	2900–3099	3100–3399	DL	Sept. Sun	Ash Wed	East. Sun	Asc. Thu	Pent. Sun	Corp. Chr.	Adv. Sun
16	3	14		6	17		9		C							
5		3	14		6	17		9	D	Jan 18	Feb 4	Mar 22	Apr 30	May 10	May 21	Nov 29
	11		3	14		6	17		E	19	5	23	May 1	11	22	30
13		11		3	14		6	17	F	20	6	24	2	12	23	Dec 1
2	19		11		3	14		6	G	21	7	25	3	13	24	2
	8	19		11		3	14		A	22	8	26	4	14	25	3
10		8	19		11		3	14	B	23	9	27	5	15	26	Nov 27
	16		8	19		11		3	C	24	10	28	6	16	27	28
18	5	16		8	19		11		D	25	11	29	7	17	28	29
7		5	16		8	19		11	E	26	12	30	8	18	29	30
	13		5	16		8	19		F	27	13	31	9	19	30	Dec 1
15	2	13		5	16		8	19	G	28	14	Apr 1	10	20	31	2
4		2	13		5	16		8	A	29	15	2	11	21	Jun 1	3
	10		2	13		5	16		B	30	16	3	12	22	2	Nov 27
12		10		2	13		5	16	C	31	17	4	13	23	3	28
1	18		10		2	13		5	D	Feb 1	18	5	14	24	4	29
	7	18		10		2	13		E	2	19	6	15	25	5	30
9		7	18		10		2	13	F	3	20	7	16	26	6	Dec 1
	15		7	18		10		2	G	4	21	8	17	27	7	2
17	4	15		7	18		10		A	5	22	9	18	28	8	3
6		4	15		7	18		10	B	6	23	10	19	29	9	Nov 27
	12		4	15		7	18		C	7	24	11	20	30	10	28
14	1	12		4	15		7	18	D	8	25	12	21	31	11	29
3		1	12		4	15		7	E	9	26	13	22	Jun 1	12	30
	9		1	12		4	15		F	10	27	14	23	2	13	Dec 1
11		9		1	12		4	15	G	11	28	15	24	3	14	2
	17		9		1	12		4	A	12	Mar 1	16	25	4	15	3
19	6	17	17	9		1	12	12	B	13	2	17	26	5	16	Nov 27
8	14	6	6	17	9	9	1	1	C	14	3	18	27	6	17	28
									D	15	4	19	28	7	18	29
									E	16	5	20	29	8	19	30
									F	17	6	21	30	9	20	Dec 1
									G	18	7	22	31	10	21	2
									A	19	8	23	Jun 1	11	22	3
									B	20	9	24	2	12	23	Nov 27
									C	21	10	25	3	13	24	28

Arguments: Golden Numbers and Dominical Letters
Explanation in *Section 28*.

TABLE XIX
Annual Martyrology Letters

800–1099	1100–1399	1400–1582	1582–1699	1700–1899	1900–2199	2200–2299 / 2400–2499	2300–2399 / 2500–2599	2600–2899	2900–3099	3100–3399	Mart Let
GN		16									G
	16	5									F
16	5										E
5		13									D
	13	2									C
13	2										B
2		10									A
	10										u
10		18									t
	18	7									s
18	7		16								r
7		15	5	16							q
	15	4		5	16						p
15	4		13		5	16					n
4		12	2	13		5	16				m
	12	1		2	13		5	16			l
12	1		10		2	13		5	16		k
1		9		10		2	13		5	16	i
	9		18		10		2	13		5	h
9		17	7	18		10		2	13		g
	17	6		7	18		10		2	13	f
17	6		15		7	18		10		2	e
6		14	4	15		7	18		10		d
	14	3		4	15		7	18		10	c
14	3		12		4	15		7	18		b
3		11	1	12		4	15		7	18	a
	11			1	12		4	15		7	P
11		19	9		1	12		4	15		N
	19	8		9		1	12		4	15	M
19	8		17		9		1	12		4	H
8			6	17		9		1	12		G
				6	17[F]		9		1	12[F]	F
			14		6	17		9		1	E
			3	14		6	17		9		D
				3	14		6	17		9	C
			11		3	14		6	17		B
				11		3	14		6	17	A
			19		11		3	14		6	u
			8	19		11		3	14		t
				8	19		11		3	14	s
					8	19		11		3	r
						8	19		11		q
							8	19		11	p
								8	19		n
									8	19	m
										8	l

Argument: Golden Numbers

Explanation in *Section 29.*

TABLE XX

List of Movable Feasts

Year	GN	DL	Mart. Let.	Sept. Sun.	Ash Wed.	East. Sun.	Asc. Thu.	Pent. Sun.	Corp. Chr.	Adv. Sun.
1941	4	E	b	Feb 9	Feb 26	Apr 13	May 22	Jun 1	Jun 12	Nov 30
1942	5	D	n	Feb 1	Feb 18	Apr 5	May 14	May 24	Jun 4	Nov 29
1943	6	C	E	Feb 21	Mar 10	Apr 25	Jun 3	Jun 13	Jun 24	Nov 28
1944	7	BA	e	Feb 6	Feb 23	Apr 9	May 18	May 28	Jun 8	Dec 3
1945	8	G	r	Jan 28	Feb 14	Apr 1	May 10	May 20	May 31	Dec 2
1946	9	F	H	Feb 17	Mar 6	Apr 21	May 30	Jun 9	Jun 20	Dec 1
1947	10	E	h	Feb 2	Feb 19	Apr 6	May 15	May 25	Jun 5	Nov 30
1948	11	DC	u	Jan 25	Feb 11	Mar 28	May 6	May 16	May 27	Nov 28
1949	12	B	P	Feb 13	Mar 2	Apr 17	May 26	Jun 5	Jun 16	Nov 27
1950	13	A	l	Feb 5	Feb 22	Apr 9	May 18	May 28	Jun 8	Dec 3
1951	14	G	C	Jan 21	Feb 7	Mar 25	May 3	May 13	May 24	Dec 2
1952	15	FE	c	Feb 10	Feb 27	Apr 13	May 22	Jun 1	Jun 12	Nov 30
1953	16	D	p	Feb 1	Feb 18	Apr 5	May 14	May 24	Jun 4	Nov 29
1954	17	C	[F]	Feb 14	Mar 3	Apr 18	May 27	Jun 6	Jun 17	Nov 28
1955	18	B	f	Feb 6	Feb 23	Apr 10	May 19	May 29	Jun 9	Nov 27
1956	19	AG	s	Jan 29	Feb 15	Apr 1	May 10	May 20	May 31	Dec 2
1957	1	F	N	Feb 17	Mar 6	Apr 21	May 30	Jun 9	Jun 20	Dec 1
1958	2	E	k	Feb 2	Feb 19	Apr 6	May 15	May 25	Jun 5	Nov 30
1959	3	D	B	Jan 25	Feb 11	Mar 29	May 7	May 17	May 28	Nov 29
1960	4	CB	b	Feb 14	Mar 2	Apr 17	May 26	Jun 5	Jun 16	Nov 27
1961	5	A	n	Jan 29	Feb 15	Apr 2	May 11	May 21	Jun 1	Dec 3
1962	6	G	E	Feb 18	Mar 7	Apr 22	May 31	Jun 10	Jun 21	Dec 2
1963	7	F	e	Feb 10	Feb 27	Apr 14	May 23	Jun 2	Jun 13	Dec 1
1964	8	ED	r	Jan 26	Feb 12	Mar 29	May 7	May 17	May 28	Nov 29
1965	9	C	H	Feb 14	Mar 3	Apr 18	May 27	Jun 6	Jun 17	Nov 28
1966	10	B	h	Feb 6	Feb 23	Apr 10	May 19	May 29	Jun 9	Nov 27
1967	11	A	u	Jan 22	Feb 8	Mar 26	May 4	May 14	May 25	Dec 3
1968	12	GF	P	Feb 11	Feb 28	Apr 14	May 23	Jun 2	Jun 13	Dec 1
1969	13	E	l	Feb 2	Feb 19	Apr 6	May 15	May 25	Jun 5	Nov 30
1970	14	D	C	Jan 25	Feb 11	Mar 29	May 7	May 17	May 28	Nov 29
1971	15	C	c	Feb 7	Feb 24	Apr 11	May 20	May 30	Jun 10	Nov 28
1972	16	BA	p	Jan 30	Feb 16	Apr 2	May 11	May 21	Jun 1	Dec 3
1973	17	G	[F]	Feb 18	Mar 7	Apr 22	May 31	Jun 10	Jun 21	Dec 2
1974	18	F	f	Feb 10	Feb 27	Apr 14	May 23	Jun 2	Jun 13	Dec 1
1975	19	E	s	Jan 26	Feb 12	Mar 30	May 8	May 18	May 29	Nov 30
1976	1	DC	N	Feb 15	Mar 3	Apr 18	May 27	Jun 6	Jun 17	Nov 28
1977	2	B	k	Feb 6	Feb 23	Apr 10	May 19	May 29	Jun 9	Nov 27
1978	3	A	B	Jan 22	Feb 8	Mar 26	May 4	May 14	May 25	Dec 3
1979	4	G	b	Feb 11	Feb 28	Apr 15	May 24	Jun 3	Jun 14	Dec 2
1980	5	FE	n	Feb 3	Feb 20	Apr 6	May 15	May 25	Jun 5	Nov 30

APPENDIX

Passover in the years AD 25 to 33

IN PROJECTING a lunar calendar, either Jewish or Gregorian, into the remote past, the following may be taken as initial dates: 1845, Oct 1.655, which is the autumnal mean new moon appertaining to 1 Tishri, and 1845, Mar 8.941, the vernal mean new moon appertaining to Easter.

The initial date is first brought down to some suitable following year (*Section 22*) by the use of the 19-year period with its subtrahend of 0.312, or by the use of the annual terms:

$$-10.633 \qquad +18.898 \qquad -11.633 \qquad +17.898$$

A suitable interval is then subtracted to arrive at the desired former year, and the proper term is applied to obtain the corresponding mean new moon date. The day of the month thus obtained is a New Style date; it may be converted into the corresponding Old Style date, if before 1582, by applying to it a correction taken from the Table here given.

CONVERSION OF NS DATES (DAY OF MONTH) INTO OS DATES

Periods	Corr.	Periods	Corr.
1500–1582, Oct 14	−10 days	600–699	−3 days
1400–1499	−9	500–599	−2
1300–1399	−8	300–499	−1
1100–1299	−7	200–299	0
1000–1099	−6	100–199	+1
900– 999	−5	AD 0– 99	+2
700– 899	−4		

In the reversed use of the 76-year interval the term is +0.24728, and the computer must subtract one day for every Gregorian century common year (listed below) that he crosses. The following Table of multiples of the 76-year interval and their corresponding terms will greatly simplify the work.

It will sometimes happen that of two neighboring mean new moons there will be doubt which should be taken. In the Gregorian lunar calendar the range of the calendar Easter new moon (Mar 8 to Apr 5, both dates included) will usually remove the doubt, and in all cases the use of Table XVIII with the year's golden number and dominical letter will decide which is the Easter new moon. In the Jewish calendar the range of 1 Tishri (Sep 5 to Oct 5, both included) will usually decide which autumnal mean new moon appertains to 1 Tishri; if the doubt still persists, recourse must be had to a table, not here given, of embolismic years proper to the various periods. In the first century of our Era, the years having the Jewish golden numbers: 2, 5, 8, 11, 13, 16, 19 are embolismic, that is, they contain (13×29.53) or 383 to 385 days each; the remaining years are called ordinary and contain (12×29.53) or 353 to 355 days.

Interval	Term	Interval	Term
76 yrs.	+0.247	988	+3.215
152	0.495	1064	3.462
228	0.742	1140	3.709
304	0.989	1216	3.956
380	1.236	1292	4.204
456	1.484	1368	4.451
532	1.731	1444	4.698
608	1.978	1520	4.946
684	2.226	1596	5.193
760	2.473	1672	5.440
836	2.720	1748	5.687
912	2.967	1824	5.935

Gregorian Century Common Years	
AD 100	AD 1000
200	1100
300	1300
500	1400
600	1500
700	1700
900	1800

The adjustable civil calendar at the end of this book will be very convenient in determining the day of the week. The dominical letter to be used as index, if before 1582, is the one found by the Old Style formula of *Section 3*.

The beginning of the Jewish year (in autumn), or 1 Tishri, is the proper autumnal mean new moon day itself; but the following day must be taken, if the new moon day

1° has the decimal 0.75 or larger;

2° is a Sunday, Wednesday, or Friday;

3° is a Monday after an embolismic year and has the decimal 0.646435 or larger;

4° is a Tuesday before an ordinary year and has the decimal 0.38287 or larger.

But if that following day is a Sunday, Wednesday, or Friday, the next day must be taken, thus causing a lag of two days behind the autumnal mean new moon. Similarly, any other calendar new moon depending on this 1 Tishri will have a lag of as many days behind its mean new moon.

From 1 Tishri thus determined, the Passover, or 15 Nisan, of the *preceding* Jewish year, but of the *same* Gregorian year, is found by counting back 163 days. The Table here given will facilitate this operation, and gives

Range of

1 Nisan (New Moon)		15 Nisan (Passover)		1 Tishri (New Year)
Mar 12	+ 14 =	Mar 26	+ 163 =	Sep 5
13		27		6
14		28		7
15		29		8
16		30		9
17		31		10
18		Apr 1		11
19		2		12
20		3		13
21		4		14
22		5		15
23		6		16
24		7		17
25		8		18
26		9		19
27		10		20
28		11		21
29		12		22
30		13		23
31		14		24
Apr 1		15		25
2		16		26
3		17		27
4		18		28
5		19		29
6		20		30
7		21		Oct 1
8		22		2
9		23		3
10		24		4
11		25		5

the range of three important dates: 1 Nisan, 15 Nisan and 1 Tishri, all in the same Gregorian year. Since 163 exceeds the highest multiple of seven by two days, and 1 Tishri cannot fall on Sunday, Wednesday, or Friday, it follows that Passover, or 15 Nisan, can never fall on Monday, Wednesday, or Friday.

The Jewish day begins on the preceding evening shortly after sundown and ends after sundown. A Gregorian date, therefore, with the decimal 0.75 or larger must be augmented by one day to obtain its Jewish designation; thus, April 2.936 (Gregorian) is April 3 (Jewish). Before the destruction of the Temple in AD 70, and the dispersion of the Jews by the Romans, the new moons, important because of the Jewish new moon festivals, and because the Jewish yearly calendar was determined by them, were still observed from the first appearance of the apparent moon's thin sickle, and the fact was reported to the Committee of the Sanhedrin that supervised, under the chairmanship of the High Priest, the yearly calendar and its festivals. But the reports of the witnesses were controlled by secret rules* preserved in the high-priestly family.

The results of those traditional secret rules, accumulated by long experience, could not have differed substantially from those obtained by means of the present mode of computing the Jewish festivals, first published by the Patriarch Hillel II, about AD 359, and adopted between 360 and 500. National and religious calendars are not easily changed, least of all in a race so tenacious of religious traditions as is the Jewish.

Our Lord, being a Jew, would naturally accept the Jewish yearly calendar as determined by legitimate authority. However, he must have been aware of the contradiction between the Law of God in Leviticus (23:5) prescribing 14 Nisan, and the paternal traditions prescribing 15 Nisan for Passover. He had sharply rebuked the Scribes and Pharisees in a similar matter for making void the commandment of God for their tradition (Matthew 15:1–6). It is not surprising, therefore, to find that he and his disciples ate the Pasch on 14 Nisan instead of 15 Nisan. There were doubtless others, similarly zealous for the Law, who ate the Pasch on 14 Nisan; the owner of the dining hall already furnished (Mark 14:15) was probably one of them. They naturally also anticipated the day of Preparation for the Pasch, putting it on 13 Nisan; this was for them the first day of unleavened bread (Matthew 26:17), because a part of the Preparation consisted in removing all leaven from their homes; but the solemnity itself of unleavened bread they celebrated on 15 Nisan as the Law prescribed. (Leviticus 23:6).

To this more or less *private* celebration of the Passover on 14 Nisan the Synoptics frequently refer; the *official* celebration of the Passover was then, as now, on 15 Nisan. To this official Passover St. John refers; for he is speaking of the party of the Sanhedrin, the chief priests and ancients, the scribes and the Pharisees, who stood there before Pilate's hall as Christ's accusers.

* The High Priest doubtless applied the saros (*Section 19*), known since the Babylonian captivity (BC 606 to 536), to control the witnesses, and the Metonic cycle (*Section 23*) to determine 1 Tishri.

Their Passover, combined with the solemnity of unleavened bread (Leviticus 23:6) was to be on the morrow, that is, on 15 Nisan.

We now take up the question of finding on what day of the week Passover occurred in the years 25 to 33. We solve it in two ways corroborating each other. We project the Gregorian lunar calendar back to determine the vernal mean new moons appertaining to Easter, in those years, and by the addition of 13 days we determine the fourteenth moon; and we project the Jewish calendar back in the same way to determine 1 Tishri. A comparison

WORK SHEET

Year	Vernal Mean New Moon			Autumnal Mean New Moon			
1845		Mar 8.941	(based on Lindo)	Sep 31.655 (Lindo)			
1846		27.839		21.022			
1847		17.206		10.389			
1848L		35.104		28.287			
1849		Mar 24.471		Sep 17.654			
−1824		+5.935	reversed subtrahend	+5.935			
		−14.	from AD 25 to 1849	−14.			
		+2.	conversion to OS dates	+2.			
	DL		14th Moon		D_w	1 Tishri	15 Nisan
AD 25	G	Mar 18.406 + 13	Sat, Mar 31	Sep 11.589	Tue	Tue, Sep 11	Sun, Apr 1
26	F	37.304*	Fri, Apr 19	30.487	Mon	Mon, Sep 30	Sat, Apr 20
27	E	26.671	Tue, Apr 8	19.854	Fri	Sat, Sep 20	Thu, Apr 10
28L	DC	15.038	Sun, Mar 28	8.221	Wed	Thu, Sep 9	Tue, Mar 30
29	B	33.936	Fri, Apr 15	27.119	Tue	Tue, Sep 27	Sun, Apr 17
30	A	23.303	Wed, Apr 5	16.486	Sat	Sat, Sep 16	Thu, Apr 6
31	G	12.670	Sun, Mar 25	5.853	Wed	Thu, Sep 6	Tue, Mar 27
32L	FE	30.568	Sat, Apr 12	23.751	Tue	Thu, Sep 25	Tue, Apr 15
33	D	19.935	Wed, Apr 1	13.118	Sun	Mon, Sep 14	Sat, Apr 4

* After adding one lunation (29.531 days) to bring its 14th moon into the *same* lunation that contains 15 Nisan, as derived from 1 Tishri.

of the fourteenth moon thus found, with 15 Nisan, as derived from 1 Tishri, will then show the shift of the latter date due to the peculiar Jewish way of determining the beginning of their year.

A beginning is made with the two standard dates in AD 1845 above mentioned, and they are both carried forward to 1849. See the work sheet.

A very large interval of 1824 years is next applied in reverse; its term of 5.935 days must be added; 14 days must be subtracted corresponding to the Gregorian century common years in the interval AD 25 to 1849 (100, 200, 300, etc.); a correction of plus two days must be applied for the first century to convert all following dates into Old Style dates. The resulting two mean new moons of AD 25, viz., Mar 18.406 and Sep 11.589 are carried forward to AD 33.

The fourteenth moon is next found from each of the vernal new moons by the addition of 13 days, and the Old Style dominical letters are computed to determine with the adjustable civil calendar the day of the week on which the fourteenth moon falls, as also to determine the day of the week (D_W) on which the autumnal mean new moon falls in each of these nine years. Then the rules for finding 1 Tishri are applied, and finally 15 Nisan (163 days earlier) and its day of the week is determined.

It must be remembered that, not the fourteenth moon thus found, but 15 Nisan, determined from 1 Tishri, is the official Jewish Passover.

In our problem of selecting possible years for Christ's death, four conditions must be fulfilled.

1° Christ ate the Pasch on Thursday evening (Matthew 26:20). This follows from the sequence of events narrated by all four Evangelists—the last supper and the capture on Thursday; the trial, crucifixion, and burial on Friday; the sealing of the tomb and stationing of guards on Saturday; the resurrection on Sunday.

2° On Friday morning the Jews would not enter Pilate's hall, lest they be defiled and prevented from eating the Pasch (John 18:28).

3° Friday was "the Preparation of the Pasch" (John 19:14; Luke 23:54), for which reason Saturday, beginning Friday evening after sundown, is called "a great Sabbath" (John 19:31) or "most solemn" (Leviticus 23:7), combining as it did that year, the weekly Sabbath with the official Passover and the solemnity of unleavened bread.

4° Sunday, the first day of the week, beginning Saturday evening, was not a day of rest; for the pious women (Luke 23:54ff.), having prepared spices and ointments on the day of the Preparation as the Sabbath drew on (Friday before sundown), and having rested on the Sabbath day (Saturday) "according to the commandment," came to the sepulchre very early in the morning of the first day of the week (Sunday) bringing the spices which they had prepared. Therefore, the official Passover combined with the solemnity of the unleavened bread (15 Nisan) could not have occurred on that Sunday, for it would have been a day of rest. (Leviticus 23:7.)

That defilement, the fear of which kept the Jews from entering Pilate's hall on Friday morning, was not an ordinary levitical uncleanness that would have ceased at sundown. Familiarity with Gentiles is not in the list of defilements given in Leviticus. It was regarded as something far worse—

apostasy from the race—like the sin of the publicans who collected taxes from their fellow Jews for the Romans. (Matthew 9:11.) Both classes were "excommunicati vitandi," like lepers, and needed a public reconciliation. (Cf. Mark 1:44; Acts 10:28.)

We shall now discuss the single years in question, with the work sheet before us.

AD 25. This year is certainly excluded by the fourth condition, however one may argue about the first three conditions. Passover combined with the solemnity of the unleavened bread (15 Nisan) on Sunday, Apr. 1 would have been a day of rest.

AD 26. This might well have been the year of Christ's death. All four conditions are fulfilled. The last supper would have taken place on Thursday evening, Apr 18, when the Jewish Friday, Apr 19, or 14 Nisan had already begun. The official Passover, or 15 Nisan, was on Saturday, Apr 20, beginning Friday evening after sundown. St. John's remarks would be perfectly applicable to this year.

AD 27. The missing day between the fourteenth moon on Tuesday, Apr 8, derived from the vernal mean new moon, and 15 Nisan on Thursday, Apr 10, derived from the autumnal new moon, is due to the lag of one day in the determination of 1 Tishri.

This is an impossible year because the official Pasch was over by Thursday evening, Apr 10. The first three conditions are not fulfilled.

AD 28. The missing day between Sunday, Mar 28 and Tuesday, Mar 30, is due to a lag of one day in the determination of 1 Tishri.

This is an impossible year; the official Pasch would have been over by Tuesday evening, Mar 30. The first three conditions are not fulfilled.

AD 29. The decimal 0.936 of the vernal mean new moon, larger than 0.75, shows that the Passover new moon festival was on Apr 3 (Jewish), and that Saturday, Apr 16, thirteen days later, was 14 Nisan.

This is an impossible year, like AD 25; the fourth condition is not fulfilled.

AD 30. An impossible year for reasons given in AD 27.

AD 31. The missing day between Sunday, Mar 25, and Tuesday, Mar 27, is due to a lag of one day in the determination of 1 Tishri.

An impossible year for reasons given in AD 28.

AD 32. The two missing days between Saturday, Apr 12, and Tuesday, Apr 15 are due to a lag of two days in the determination of 1 Tishri.

An impossible year for reasons given in AD 28.

AD 33. The two missing days between Wednesday, Apr 1, and Saturday, Apr 4, are accounted for as follows: The decimal 0.935, larger than 0.75, shows that the Passover mean new moon in this year was on Mar 20 (Jewish). The 15 Nisan on Saturday, Apr 4, derived from 1 Tishri, shows that the Passover *calendar* new moon, or 1 Nisan, was on Mar 21 (see table given above), with a consequent lag of one day behind the Passover mean new moon, due to a lag of one day in the determination of 1 Tishri. The addition of 13 days puts 14 Nisan on Friday, Apr 3.

This might have been the year of the crucifixion. Mar 21 (Jewish) was the Passover new moon festival, and 14 Nisan, 13 days later, was Friday, Apr 3, beginning Thursday evening, Apr 2, after sundown, when Christ could have eaten the Pasch with his disciples in strict conformity with God's Law in Leviticus 23:5. The Jews, following their paternal traditions, celebrated the official Passover combined with the solemnity of the unleavened bread (Leviticus 23:6) on 15 Nisan which was Saturday, Apr 4. All four conditions are fulfilled.

The results of the investigation are:

1° Of the nine years considered, only AD 26 or 33 could have been the year of Christ's death.

2° Both the last supper and the crucifixion took place on 14 Nisan, which should have been the Jewish Passover according to Leviticus 23:5.

3° The resurrection occurred either on Sunday, Apr 21 of the year 26, or on Sunday, Apr 5 of the year 33.

INDEX

(References are to pages)